LIQUID SOFTWARE

How to Achieve Trusted Continuous Updates
in the DevOps World

Fred Simon, Yoav Landman, Baruch Sadogursky

Title: Liquid Software
ISBN: 13: 978-1981855728
Subtitle: How to Achieve Trusted Continuous Updates in the DevOps World
Authors: Fred Simon, Yoav Landman, Baruch Sadogursky

To contact the authors or the copyright holder, please send an email to LSbook@jfrog.com.

To stay continuously updated on the Liquid Software Revolution of Continuous Updates please visit liquidsoftware.com.

Liquid Software is dedicated to everyone who has ever wished machines would work for us, instead of the other way around.

Acknowledgements

This book has been a journey for us. A journey that explored the present and looked into what we believe the software industry will look like in the not too distant future. A journey that has forced us to plumb the depths of our experience as we brainstormed together to shape our thoughts into a coherent vision.

Among those who joined us on the journey, we would particularly like to thank: Shlomi Ben Haim – for his total support of our vision for *Liquid Software*; Kit Merker – for his thorough review of the texts and thought provoking, insightful comments; Rami Honig and Shani Levy – for paying attention to every detail, while tirelessly driving this work to completion; and Jody Ben-David and Steve Spencer of J-R Research – for their invaluable contributions to getting our thoughts and vision down on paper. Finally, we'd like to thank all the frogs who are making the vision of liquid software a reality.

Table of Contents

THE END

We'd like to tell you that we're software soothsayers, capable of predicting with pinpoint accuracy where the industry as a whole will be ten years from now. We'd love to say that the **liquid software revolution of continuous updates with zero downtime** will lead to ponies, rainbows, and Happy Ever Afters for everyone. Of course, we can't do that.

We do know, however, that breakthroughs *can and do* occur. The kind that radically change our perceptions of the possible. The kind that fundamentally alter what we manufacture and consume. We're confident that the adoption of continuous updates will be *that* transformative. It will accelerate with the rise of cloud computing and the Internet of Things, as those and other technologies will demand it. The new normal that is still evolving includes: anywhere, anytime, always running, fully interconnected, transparent, cross-platform computing. People want every software-driven thing to seamlessly integrate with all other software-driven things.

Software already runs practically everything that keeps modern society functioning. There is, and will continue to be, demand for more software, and for software that is ever more responsive and versatile. As software becomes more complex, more mistakes will be made. Updates will need to occur with greater regularity, whether they are new functionalities or patches. The only practical way to accommodate these rising and accelerating demands is to make software more liquid.

Liquefaction also makes sense in terms of user psychology and preference. Our greatest digital achievements happen when average users don't see or concern themselves with the inner mechanics of their software-powered devices. All the engineering ingenuity and prowess stays behind the curtain in service of easy, intuitive operations. Every time we eliminate a confusing or irritating technical procedure, while delivering more and better functionality, everyone's a winner.

Consider this tremendously powerful argument in favor of liquid software: *Spectre*. Publicly disclosed in January 2018, Spectre is a vulnerability that affects microprocessors that perform branch prediction. It fools computer and device applications into accessing arbitrary sectors of their memory space. This gives attackers the ability to read that memory and potentially obtain sensitive data. It's extremely pernicious, and its impacts are far-reaching. All current CPU architectures are vulnerable! Darkest of all, there's no protection against it. Spectre-based exploits are only discoverable *after* they've been applied and the damage has been done. That's the kind of five-alarm fire that demands rapid response. Continuous updates are currently the quickest and best way to solve the problem – securely, and without incurring downtime.

Barriers to the acceptance and implementation of liquid software are multi-faceted – the most significant being developers' unfamiliarity with continuous update methodologies and the DevOps practices that we believe are fundamental to ensuring success. Even those who do have some knowledge of these matters have concerns. Everyone in the industry would like to provide updates with greater speed, flexibility, and transparency. So, conceptually, liquid software scores big points. The issue is how to achieve these goals and deliver software that's secure and able to maintain high levels of uninterrupted productivity. Do we keep nursing along legacies, or do we become the pioneers of innovation?

Blazing new trails is in the nature of things. These are next generation software ideas. And new generations are often prepared to work in fundamentally different ways than those that have preceded them. They dream of things that never were. Their motto is: If it ain't broke, break it! That's how new paradigms are born.

Let the revolution begin!

Fred Simon
Yoav Landman
Baruch Sadogursky

May 2018

CHAPTER 1:
THE ROAD TO DISRUPTION

*"Learning and innovation go hand in hand.
The arrogance of success is to think that what you did
yesterday will be sufficient for tomorrow."*
– William G. Pollard, physicist

Not Your Father's Software Release

Changes in the ways software, and software updates, are conceived, developed, and deployed – and in the nature of how software operates – are changing the way R&D works. Continuous improvement is the goal. To achieve this, the era of big releases is coming to an end.

Continuous improvement is not only about continuous development and deployment of software. It is an adjustment to how the marketplace operates. For the past several decades, software has been sold as a commodity, or a good. A customer would pay a price to own a license for a piece of software or a software package. Revenue generated would be immediately transactional, with customers paying directly to acquire it. The marketplace is shifting, and it will continue to shift away from this model toward one in which software consumption is fluid and revenues are generated not as one-time payments, but as a constant stream, as users access a software *service*. This is particularly significant for newer software vendors. If large upfront sums of cash are no longer secured through big major releases, it becomes more difficult to set aside necessary sums for personnel-heavy and capital-intensive research and development (R&D) and quality assurance (QA). The push, then, is toward continuous improvement that can coexist alongside development.

This concept is not to be confused with continuous deployment, which is usually associated with installing new versions to runtimes in data centers and production systems that are strictly under a given company's control. In that environment, it is usually taken for granted that each company will have a firm grasp and understanding of the runtimes to which deployments are being pushed. **Continuous updating that produces continual improvement** is the rational expansion of this approach. This means establishing the reliable and secure manner by which companies handle runtimes that they can push updates to, or pull updates from. It's a paradigm shift that's already underway.

This radical, yet highly logical response to the challenges of our increasingly software-driven world is the **liquid software revolution**.

LATE 1990s

MID 2000s

MID 2010s

NOW

The Evolution of Mobile Updates

Liquid Software?

In the traditional software scenario, an update is developed, delivered, and installed as an individual stand-alone item. It arrives as a neat little (or big) file which thousands – or even millions – of users open, and voila –

there's the update. Continuous, fluid (liquid) delivery and deployment of updates, on the other hand, is like the constant, unending flow of a stream or river. It includes the monitoring of this flow, and unceasing interactivity with the software that is being continuously updated.

Liquid software is able to continuously update itself because it's simultaneously impacting and communicating data from something that is already running and in use by end-users. How those customers use and interact with their software will evidence new demands, unforeseen limitations, and other issues, which establish the basis for software to be improved by way of adjustments or the addition of new features.

While of course a discrete system undergirds it, liquid software is made up of tiny pieces, like drops of water make up the ocean. And there are so many of these pieces that it becomes no longer possible for any single person to distinguish individual components. The liquid software revolution now taking place is the transition from transferring packages to transferring micro-deltas of software. This order of magnitude advancement in software DevOps is being spurred on by a world that needs software (and software companies) to be ever more responsive to market demands, and disruptive of old (non-informed) ways of doing things. Development, testing, distribution, and implementation processes are getting faster and faster, with smaller and smaller bits being delivered to more and more environments.

We have reached the stage where the creation, bundling, transmission, and installation of big packages are impediments to business growth and productivity. As well, the ability of government, NGOs, and other service providers to assist more people, and to operate more efficiently, is restrained. This is keeping all of us from using and updating everyday device software in what could be an almost completely transparent manner. Our present experiences make us desire a world in which continuous-and-seamless is the norm. While most users are unaware of it, our collective expectations are fueling the liquid software revolution.

This is not to suggest that we should plunge headlong into this future, ignoring the challenges that liquid updates can present. We can't ignore the way we humans absorb changes. There's no sense or purpose in pushing modifications that disrupt the present expectations of users. As ingenious and cutting edge as we can be on the technological side of things, we need to be every bit as clever in the ways we handle user experience, change management, feature promotion, training and support services, etc. Such concerns won't apply to every release, but they'll certainly pertain to those that are most likely to be disruptive. These, in particular, should be thought of as design constraints that give us pause to consider whether the adoption costs associated with an improvement can really be justified. Optimally, new features should be designed to be intuitive, requiring zero training; they should feel natural, as if they've always been here, just waiting for users to discover them. This approach will improve performance and connectivity, and ultimately lead to software that's faster, more secure, and easier to navigate.

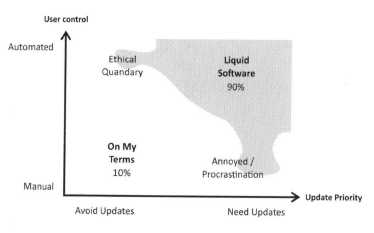

Driving Forces Behind Liquid Software

The Source (Code) of Liquidity

The drive toward liquidity is fueled by user needs and desires as well as by the software developer community. Much of this drive has come about because more developers are becoming involved with open source projects. As these people communicate and create code together, the nature of the processes in which they are engaged represent a stark example of how software can be developed more quickly and in a profoundly more efficient and inventive manner than can be accomplished in a tech firm's office. These software craftspeople – through their easy access to better tools at home – have established the framework for how software can and should be created, built, and distributed in the future.

And let's be crystal clear. We're not waxing poetic about the creativity of DevOps professionals, or positing academic notions about efficiency. The liquid software revolution is as much about return on investment as it is about radically transforming processes. Companies create software to assist customers to achieve goals, and if they get the job done right, their bottom lines will reflect that success. Increasingly, doing it right is seen as the adoption of small, efficient methods pioneered in the open source community. Large software firms are realizing that the path to better software and greater profit is through the establishment of a continual feedback process between their enterprise customers (and end-users in general) and the software they are creating. Building the pipelines (the liquid software infrastructure) and the management systems for ongoing, continuous operations can dramatically shorten the time span between perceiving user needs that should be accommodated (or detecting bugs that require patching), and making software improvements. This overall improvement in quality, and the consistent delivery of continuous improvements, will be rewarded. Software companies that join the liquid software revolution will see their costs decline and their productivity, marketplace respect, and profits increase.

As we have seen with many innovations in many different industries, change is not always immediate, nor is it always rapidly embraced. Large software companies have entrenched cultures and ways of doing business that often have evolved over the course of many years. It's frequently not enough for an innovation to present itself as a great creative idea or even a new approach that's winning the hearts and minds of the geek class. It's the real, tangible results being produced by liquid software revolutionaries that are now motivating the industry as a whole to pay attention to what's happening, and in a desire not to be left behind, to learn what they need to do to transform their own operations.

An especially interesting aspect of the liquid software revolution is the cross-boundary nature of the developer community. Developers are moving from industry to industry, sharing their knowledge and their craft with their developer peers, whether those individuals are working in the automotive, manufacturing, or retail world. It's not about a specific, industrial goal, but rather about how developers – all developers – are creating software. We are now experiencing a wave of cross-industry adoption of new DevOps practices, tools, and technologies. It's reached the point where every industry – and even every company – knows it must ride this wave. Those already on board are benefiting from making the shift, and many others are acknowledging the need to move in this direction.

When Software Starts to Wilt

Software is everywhere. And *every* company is a software company. The trend toward the digitalization of anything and everything is growing rapidly. This trend shows every sign of continuing into the foreseeable future, and beyond. We see this exponential growth particularly in the Internet of Things (IoT), where devices, home appliances, automobiles, and so much more, are already or are soon to become a part of our "smart" world of electronics. People are becoming accustomed to devices that respond to their behaviors, and that respond situationally to the environments in which they operate. In the coming new normal, the digital adjuncts of daily life will routinely function in the ways individuals and businesses want them to. In this new normal, users will instinctively wonder why a particular functionality is not performing as well as it might or is not available at all. This need for software to quickly adapt to immediate circumstances, and to practically intuit what will best serve situations yet to come, cannot be adequately addressed even at the current state of software evolution, where continuous *deployments* are quite common, but continuous *updates* are not.

When Software Can't Adapt to Changing Environments

The continuous deployment of software versions is often seen today, particularly with mobile devices. Apps running on these devices are frequently being updated, which is an advancement that assures enhanced quality, as user needs and software issues are being handled with increased speed.

However, for the most part, the actual changes from one version release to the next are getting smaller and smaller. Furthermore, the software being updated is generally operating on a production runtime with existing data and live requests. The liquid software revolution is intensely concerned with the miniaturization of these updates — creating the mechanisms by which improvements, adjustments, and patches can instantly be incorporated into running systems.

We might conceptualize this in terms of a bouquet of flowers that we purchase to beautify a room. Once set in a vase of water, our bouquet has been installed and deployed. Through time and exposure to its environment, the bouquet will change. The normal and anticipated process of aging and decay will take place, making the bouquet less "functional". The useful life of the bouquet might be prematurely cut short simply because one or two individual flowers within the presentation become less attractive.

In this bouquet runtime scenario, what if we could make the bouquet self-perpetuating? What if every time a flower in that vase began to lose its appeal, it would instantly be renewed? What if the vase's water supply was continuously replenished? We, the users of the flower arrangement, would no longer have to tend to it. Everything would be done for us. Our purpose would be served, and we could go about our other business.

Software That Never Wilts

What might happen if this newfangled bouquet technology – let's call it *eBouquet* – was really a thing, right now? It is likely that we would see the rapid adoption of eBouquet and a decline in marketplace interest in the older bouquet technology, and its innovations would become the norm. This might well inspire the market to wonder what if, instead of individual flowers in an arrangement auto-rejuvenating themselves, those flowers could automatically be replaced by different flowers. Maybe the arrangement could be programmed to slowly morph into a new arrangement. The new one might be more appropriate for a particular occasion or time of year. We could well imagine many more conceptual variations.

This metaphor illustrates something inherent in the human condition. Sure, necessity is the mother of invention

– but some of the world's most interesting, compelling, and useful advances have come from creative minds giving people things they never knew they wanted. At minimum, those innovators tapped into a general (sometimes unarticulated) sense that if we can already do one thing well, surely we should be able to do something else that builds on how far we have come.

It is precisely the same with software. The further down the road we go in terms of what software can do for us, the more intense is our desire for it to do more. This is a perfectly normal impulse. How often and in how many different ways since the Industrial Revolution has some grand innovation inspired people to exclaim, "I can't imagine how we lived all this time without [insert new wonder of the world here]!"

We've arrived at a moment in time where our expectations and assumptions about what software should do demand that we move beyond the deployment and lifecycle of traditional "bouquets". Greater progress and convenience intensify the desire for more of both. Users increasingly believe that their devices should operate in certain ways and that particular functionalities should be rapidly available to them as a matter of course. It will be impossible to make those beliefs manifest without continuous updates.

Naturally, before we can know where we are heading, we have to understand where we have been.

DevOps Rules! (At Least It Should)

The sudden, gargantuan demand for IoT devices has revealed just how far away we are from being able to deliver seamless, responsive, flexible, almost intuitive continuous updates. At present, most IoT devices have very low update rates. While the firmware in smart watches and fitness trackers may be updated every few weeks, updates are fewer and farther between for smart home HVAC systems, smart TVs, health monitoring equipment in hospitals, and NASA space vehicles. Additionally, there are substantial issues related to security and trust, with failures occurring regularly. Hackers seeking to establish new and improper gateways to the Internet are routinely attacking IoT devices. In some instances, hacks are shockingly simple to execute, including some that cannot be reversed through a software patch, requiring customers to send their devices away for dedicated, hands-on, professional care.

Confronted with this, some manufacturers have chosen to hide behind the expectations people have of hardware refresh cycles, which are far less demanding than software update cycles, never mind continuous updates. These companies know that problems exist and that the bad street buzz generated by these problems is costing them business. So, what do they do? They either make it so inconvenient to update device software that users don't bother, or they stop providing updates altogether. Consider a smart TV that offers an update as an app is being launched, but allows the user to skip the update and launch the app anyway. The message on the screen doesn't explain what's in the update, why it should be installed, or how it could be installed when the TV is not being used. In this scenario, the odds are high that the average user will close the update message and go back to what they were doing.

Of course, this is not a practical solution in the short term, nor is it a sensible one in the long term, because the pressure to update will remain and only get stronger by the day. There's a tremendous tug of war going on now between end-users desiring the immediate ability to connect IoT devices to one another and to other networked devices, and the fact that the updates these devices receive are still not secure, transparent, or reliable. Moreover, even if we could tag an update as secure, a security flaw might be discovered following release, with no mitigation option possible other than a patch or a dreaded device recall. All of this leaves software manufacturers only one prudent option – to embrace the liquid software revolution.

The transformation we envision isn't the acceptance of continuous updates as an abstract notion. A company can affirm the wisdom of moving in this direction and still fail in the effort if it does not also restructure internal systems and practices. Currently, most IoT developers and the IoT community that is creating the software for these devices are *not* DevOps personnel with a DevOps mindset. They bear the heritage of hardware producers accustomed to investing lengthy periods of time in production. They believe that any post-production updates, such as patches, can be inherently risky and are to be avoided. For many, DevOps is still a new concept. Still, whether through training, conferences, trade publications, peer or market pressures, DevOps *must* be a part of every IoT firm's business plan.

This should not be a tremendous hurdle to overcome. It's just applying to IoT environments and systems the same processes and techniques that are already in place at big web and web server companies. Among other things, it's creating QA testing tools, build tools, validation tools, promotion tools, signed software pipelines – indeed everything that is discussed throughout the book you are now reading. Nevertheless, some will need a little added incentive to get them to where they need to be; where sturdy, bottom line business sense dictates that they ought to be.

Consider this: In 1993, AT&T launched a series of sophisticated television ads, all of which posed provocative, "Have you ever..." questions, such as "Have you ever watched a movie you wanted to, the minute you wanted to?" "Have you ever kept an eye on your home when you're not at home?" and "Have you ever carried your medical history in your wallet?" The tag line for each of these commercials was,

"You will." And of course – every one of those prophecies have come to pass.

We'd like to be just as clear and direct: DevOps is not the future. It's here! It's now! And it's not going away. Yes, making the shift is an investment and is not to be taken lightly. But neither is it to be ignored. Every software firm, every CEO, every business development executive, and every operations manager owes it to their company, their board, their investors, their employees, and their clients to be curious about DevOps. They should devote some reasonable amount of time to the subject, and seek out those with the knowledge and experience to assist them in getting up to speed with what DevOps is all about. Those who do may well discover that DevOps is something they can't afford not to embrace. They might even be stunned to realize that the benefits can be staggering when theirs is the company providing users with products that have the built-in solutions and the in-house know-how to reliably, continually improve lives.

We Built It, But They Didn't Come

Need still more encouragement? Well, consider the fact that secure and highly accurate updates are already being delivered through automated systems all the time. It's being done to practically every commercial airplane on the ground for servicing, to sophisticated warehousing and logistics operations, and to many modern automotive systems. Even NASA's Mars rover, *Curiosity,* received a full system upgrade from a distance of almost 140 million miles.

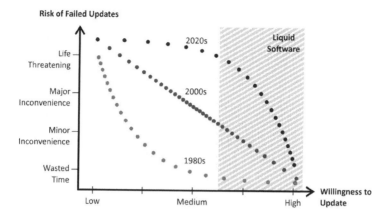

Penetration of Continuous Updates through the Decades

Of course, the fact that we have the wherewithal to do the job right doesn't always mean the job is done right. Are there examples of mishaps and failures? Certainly. But those aren't reasons to slow down the progress of the liquid software revolution and the promise of continuous updates. Rather, we should be working in an organized and resolute fashion toward globalizing and standardizing. We should be communicating to the entire software industry that updates are not something to be considered after the fact. Updates should always be part of the code that is written right from the start. Our watchcry should be: "If it's not updateable, it's not software!"

We firmly believe that the liquid software revolution will succeed in making continuous updates the norm throughout the industry. Yet we do understand that we're currently travelling through a sort of middle passage. Much of the software we all currently use (web-based and mobile apps) is, in fact, being continuously updated. These are the updates we never really think about. We see them, but their inner workings are completely transparent to us. Almost all the websites we interact with are continuously being updated, and most mobile device apps receive automatic updates, but the majority of users don't pay much attention to this. In other words, on a daily basis, users are already getting what they want and prefer – optimally functioning software with the latest feature and security updates, delivered without their having to be involved in the process. Yet for most people, the penny hasn't completely dropped. Most haven't quite reached the stage where they're wondering (or complaining) aloud about continuous update technology not being *everywhere* yet. Perhaps there would be more pressure from the market if the market was crystal clear in understanding that it could have what it wants at a significantly accelerated pace – if it would just make some noise about it. Perhaps we need to launch a high-profile advertising campaign with the tag line: "Ask your software provider if continuous updates are right for *you!*"

Whither Software Versioning

Throughout modern software history, localized installation and updating events have taken place in specific places, such as homes and offices, and on specific devices, such as PCs, laptops, servers, and mobile devices. New software and subsequent updates are assigned version numbers, which help to catalog the precise composition of any particular release of a given piece of software. These numbers are intended to highlight specific issues addressed, functionalities introduced, and patches applied. This paradigm is still very much with us today, although things are changing.

Change is evident across the landscape of mobile device apps. Many popular high-profile apps receive small updates as often as every few days. Significant change is also being driven by the fact that distributed software is becoming more common. What once was a component part of a software suite installed and running on a localized device may now be executed as a microservice that a user accesses and executes in the cloud. In this environment, individual microservices can be updated discretely according to their own independent release cycles, with no need for their deployments to be bundled into a larger package of updates with a specific version number. Although each "micro-update" alters an aggregated macro version of a given piece of software, traditional version numbering is no longer an effective or meaningful way to reflect each and every minute change that takes place. This trend is dramatically on the rise with IoT introducing more new devices that are connected to the internet, the updating of which can only be efficiently managed through automatic updates requiring no human intervention.

The average user's awareness of software versioning is waning. Most software companies have embraced the fact that the vast majority of people care only about functionality and convenience. Whether for work or for leisure, users want to interact with the software in their lives only in ways that will help them to accomplish their goals. They want to *use* software, not *tend* to it. They certainly don't want to have to pay attention to its technical dimensions.

Making Informed Decisions?

Machines, not humans, need to do the logging and tracking of version numbers and software updates. They must be able to manage and adjust to a continuous liquid flow of very small packages that are continually updating software. Machines must monitor the impact such updates are having on the larger systems software operates within.

Versioning was created to assist professionals to better manage software updates. Machines, however, are more versatile at such management, as they have faster and better means of archiving and retrieving information. Machines can create versions of software packages, libraries, and applications. They can generate version numbers from many branches in parallel, and then, based on a machine-readable version, combine discrete packages into running software. And unlike humans, they have no need for text files detailing all the many versions of a piece of software that have been installed and updated on a particular platform or system.

Users and developers may not be expressing a desire for liquid software, because they are still unfamiliar with the term. They may not articulate a desire for continuous updates, but are nevertheless eager for the benefits of automation. As it is now, most users do not upgrade major software packages, particularly computer operating systems. This is due in part to their fear of being involved in processes they believe are too technical or complicated. This fear persists even though software manufacturers have taken great care to make these experiences as simple and straightforward as possible. Most people are not confident that they possess the necessary knowledge or skill to handle such upgrades. Even those with some amount of savvy have learned (through rumor, if not experience) that it is often better to hold back on installing major upgrades, since initial releases have been introduced to the marketplace when they were less than ready for prime time.

This brings us back to what most people would prefer. In principle, most would very much like to have the latest and most improved versions of the software they use. However, they want by the best technicians. They want to be able to trust that what gets delivered to them has undergone appropriate testing and validation. They want to securely receive updates that will work properly and cause little or no disruption to their daily activities. Only machines are best equipped to satisfy all of these preferences.

Isn't Continuous Deployment Enough?

Right now, the answer to that question will depend on the end-user. With every passing day, however, the answer will increasingly be "no". We have already addressed the fact that software is everywhere and that IoT is exponentially reinforcing this. There are enterprises that require their software to be operational around the clock, and many average users want the same convenience. Only continuous updates can deliver on these demands and desires, as only liquid software can provide continuous updates with zero downtime.

Another advantage afforded us by continuous updates is the opportunity to execute the odd-sounding, but very practical task of continuous downgrade. This option is highly relevant if, while a firm is running a critical operation, it suddenly detects something very wrong in a particular process. If an update had been delivered through continuous deployment, the company might be facing serious downtime and disruption of service. But the continuous downgrade procedure allows a rollback to be executed as seamlessly as an update. In a manner of thinking, it's not so much a downgrade as it is just another update, but this update is delivering a previous version of the software.

From Solid to Liquid

The demise of software versions – at least insofar as users are concerned – is already underway. And the degree to which it's happening parallels user confidence in the products and updates coming from software vendors. We see this with routers and self-updating IoT devices, and particularly with smartphones and tablets. The average user doesn't know (or care) what version of YouTube, WhatsApp, Amazon Echo, or Google Home is running. There *are* versions, but for all intents and purposes, they remain hidden. This information is pertinent to machines, not humans.

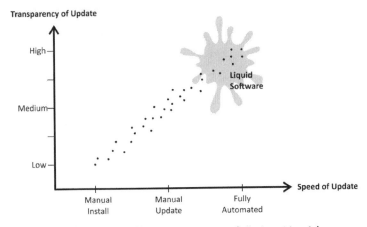

The Speed and Transparency of Going Liquid

So, we are all receiving and accepting app updates on almost a daily basis – most without the necessity for any intervention on our parts. We have confidence, at least, that software vendors are making sure that these app updates are not going to damage our devices or corrupt our personal data. The more we experience this (mobile devices and their apps serving our needs), the more we'll all be comfortable with updates taking place without our noticing.

Leaps of Faith

On our mobile devices, we typically allow app updates to be installed even when we know there will likely be no option to execute a rollback if something goes wrong. There's no user-side device testing of new version releases. They're placed directly into production with no acceptance tests needing to be run on the side. No one has a standby phone to use for the installation of new software updates.

Essentially, we're all taking an informed risk.

The risk most often encountered by running a new version of software is the loss of a functionality that we have enjoyed or relied on. Perhaps an app won't start at all because the device on which it's running has a new operating system that doesn't match the new version of the software, or the software has some other bug. Even under these circumstances, we generally don't send complaint messages to software vendors about problematic app updates. Our experience has led us to expect that the vendor will deliver a fix as soon as possible. And we're willing to incur what is rarely more than a slight disruption, even if it's quite inconvenient while we wait for the solution to arrive.

Enterprise Users: To Boldly Go...

It is possible that a user may end up with a completely malfunctioning device as a result of choosing to upgrade its operating system. For enterprise customers, however, the level of voluntary risk is, for the most part, very different. It is much more common for them to have staging servers that can test and assess the impact of upgrades. A compelling argument can be made that when the enterprise user eventually does receive a given software update, they can have a reasonable sense of security. And while most of the time this is justified, nothing's totally foolproof. Problems can definitely be revealed during staging that might not otherwise be detected. The critical factor is whether an enterprise user is well prepared to predict production problems that may occur during staging.

This places enterprise users in only a marginally better and safer position than the phone user who simply accepts any updates (whether automatic or manual) that are being fed by vendors. And while enterprise users may be able to validate some updates, they can't validate every single one. This means that, at best, new versions of enterprise software have only limited and inconsistent opportunities to be tested with real-world production loads. This places intensifying pressures on software vendors from both the consumer and enterprise segments of the market. Both groups are demanding trustworthiness, and that means vendors must ratchet up their game when it comes to validating software.

Further risks are incurred with our growing need for speed, which is fueled by the mindset and expectations of individuals in relation to their mobile devices. People are already experiencing just how quickly they can receive bug fixes and new features. So, it's natural for these same people not to understand why smooth and speedy updating cannot occur in the enterprise environment. Large firms may have the facility to carry out client-side validations that can also be automated and included as part of business-to-business, liquid software flows. However, once again, the fundamental issue here is for vendors to establish continuous update infrastructures capable of validating each and every update through necessary and appropriate testing.

A critical mass of everyday experience is pushing all levels of DevOps toward liquid software. Regardless of the software being run, regardless of the environments in which it's being run, regardless of the devices on which it's operating, regardless of whether the end-user is an individual or a corporation, we all want fluid and continuous updates.

To rapidly produce new features, bug fixes, and updated versions — few of which are overtly tangible anymore — we need to expand software capacities at a pace that is not possible to achieve via traditional updates.

It's Right Here in Front of You

Elements of a continuous update architecture *do* exist presently in large web application companies, such as Netflix, Apple, Google, Facebook, Amazon and Twitter. In these firms, from *Docker* to data center to website, liquefaction is all internal and based on proprietary systems. However, software that these companies consume from suppliers outside of those systems, as well as the software that these firms supply to external partners, is not fully liquid.

The main issue here is that DevOps is still dealing with a lot of large application packages that are not liquid. They are continuously deployed, with updates coming in the form of transfers of a lot of data and replicated services. To achieve full liquidity, continuous update systems must be able to execute continuous updates of libraries, and this will require having the concept of libraries nested within end-user devices. The way updates are currently delivered – duplicating full applications and data – is a huge waste of storage and network resources. So, once again, it's IoT that will benefit most from this focus on library updating and it's IoT that will accelerate the liquid software revolution. From advancements in IoT, the mobile device marketplace will catch on, with significant effort concentrated on continuous updates for cloud-distributed apps. Successes on these fronts will then spread across the entirety of the software development spectrum.

Flight Risk?

"Passengers, this is your captain speaking. We've reached a cruising altitude of 30,000 feet and in just a few minutes, we'll commence a software update of this airliner's major flight systems." Upon hearing such an announcement, most people might pause momentarily while absorbing the information, and then reactions could range from mild disquiet to panic.

So, let's start with the obvious question: Why the heck would anyone want to do this with an airplane, en route, carrying several hundred souls? Surely the risks involved outweigh any potential benefit? Well, before we address these questions, it should be noted that it's quite common today for airline companies to execute software updates for non-critical systems while their planes are on the ground (e.g., in-flight entertainment services, Wi-Fi, corded phones, and mobile device connectivity).

Let's return, though, to our "scary" scenario and consider a bit of context. The U.S. Federal Aviation Administration (FAA) has been working with the airline industry for several years toward the implementation of a collision detection system update. The concept is to use high-level GPS instead of radar systems to track the precise location of all planes in the sky. The coordinates provided by the GPS system would allow for significantly improved management of flights, enabling more planes to take off and land, particularly those that service crowded urban hubs. However, this kind of technology opens up the possibility that further down the line a malicious GPS spoofing hack could be discovered in GPS processing software. The upload of such bad data could penetrate an airplane's software systems, giving a bad actor control of the aircraft. An in-flight software update could avert a potentially catastrophic event by removing the vulnerable GPS processing software. After an event like that, proponents of never updating software when a plane is flying will have a hard time arguing their case.

If You Love Control, Set It Free

As we've established, with the ongoing and exponential rise in software-driven, software-managed, and software-monitored, well...everything, we have an increasing need for speed. But speed is not enough for the liquid software revolution to succeed. Current technologies allow us to rapidly accomplish a huge amount within the continuous updates arena, but we also need to establish rock solid reliability and trust in update pipelines and the data that flows back and forth between them. This is what substantially distinguishes continuous updates from continuous deployment. We typically speak of continuous deployment in terms of pushing deployments to data center and production system runtimes that are strictly under local control. As such, within many systems, we have a high level of control over the runtimes in which the software will be executed. Liquid software greatly expands the horizon because we are dealing with runtimes that can be pushed to or pulled from as part of a continuous update environment. This means we must continuously deal with runtimes that are outside of local control. When it becomes the norm for software developers and firms to confidently let go of this local control, we'll know that the liquid software era has truly arrived.

Just Sign on the Dotted Pipeline

For all that we can accomplish right now in terms of continuous updates, there are still challenges ahead. For example, API security standardization remains an issue to be overcome. In an optimal liquid software environment, the signing authority for certain types of software certification would be automated. We would be able to establish that a specific version of a specific package has been tested and validated by ABC, and passed; integration tested by XYZ, and passed; security tested by another entity, and passed. The same would occur down the line for validations of End-User License Agreements (EULAs), release and customer relationship notes, and so forth. This is yet another aspect of the engineering of completely trustworthy, worry-free pipelines. Customers wanting to obtain the latest client library and correct routing could then do so with total confidence and with full knowledge that the liquid software they receive has been properly certified and signed by all appropriate entities. The customer could then implement an automated filtering system that filters software inflow, such that they'll be receiving only that which they want. To accomplish this goal, we must build an infrastructure that establishes not only liquid communications, but also trust, between companies. This could come about through the use of certified signatures that are associated with specific types of update clusters.

Such solutions could even extend to self-driving cars, trucks, and other autonomous vehicles. However, as we might imagine, there is enormous resistance to the notion of executing continuous updates in this realm, and this resistance will likely persist for some time. While it is true in a general sense that such updates would be no different than any others, reluctance to liquefy the software governing these systems is based almost entirely on the potentially lethal results should anything go wrong.

Nevertheless, there are some current examples – Tesla is notable – of automatic updating of vehicles' self-driving features. The only difference is the amount of quality, or responsibility for quality, the vendor assumes. Some of this has to do with legal obligations and liability issues with respect to precisely who is responsible for certifying and provisioning an update. Since Tesla owners are not aware of liquid updates occurring, they cannot be held wholly responsible for a malfunction or an accident that is the result of an update. Software consumers don't have the knowledge, skills, or facilities to ascertain whether one version or another is sound and ready for deployment, nor can the owner execute appropriate and necessary rollbacks. All of that must be the sole responsibility of the vendor.

We want to state clearly that despite the fact that transportation and other high-risk industries may be averse to continuous updates, it is our belief that firms that don't embrace the liquid software revolution by implementing methodologies and systems to guarantee the quality, security, and provenance of their software, could be destined for quick demise.

We Want Information, Information, Information...

Metadata is the information that allows us to make sensible decisions about whether a piece of software and all of its component pieces are good or not. It might be metadata about the origin of a particular component, the history and features of a particular version, or validation steps that software went through – all of this and much more is critical information for a well-designed, automated pipeline. Metadata enables us to determine whether our software should or should not be promoted to the next level in a continuous integration pipeline. There's internal metadata related to our own projects, internal metadata related to other projects that we use as libraries, and external metadata related to all the components that we use. Because of the number of sources from which it can derive, our metadata can indeed be quite meta!

Ours is an age of binaries. With every software industry advancement, we've seen an exponential rise in the production of binaries. There are billions, if not trillions, of them now in play, with unknown numbers yet to come. Consequently, we emphasize in several sections of this book how and why copious amounts of highly targeted metadata are critical to the rise of the machines and the eventual success of the liquid software revolution. It's only through the robust use of metadata that we can make any sense of this vast and growing sea of artifacts. And for each artifact, we must answer questions that fall into three essential categories:

1. **Basic information**: What is it? Where did it come from? What we can do with it?

2. **Location**: What do we have, where? We have a multitude of environments – QA, pre-production, production, etc. With artifacts in every environment, we need to understand why they are where they are.

3. **Quality**: What validation did it go through and what were the results? Were Common Vulnerabilities and Exposures (CVEs) or any other bugs revealed? Was it tested internally? How did its performance test results compare to other versions of the same binary? In a continuous update system, artifacts will be generated from several different environments.

We need answers to these questions so we can make smart decisions about what should progress through our liquid software pipes at the processing phase. We must decide what should be deployed where vis-à-vis the environment from which an artifact was created.

It will be possible to address these issues only if we have enough metadata. But just how much is enough? To answer that question, let's examine security concerns related to metadata, such as CVE identifiers. And let's pretend we have an ultimate, magical solution. With a wave of our digital wand, our machine learning algorithms and big data analytics scan our source code and determine whether there are any security breaches that others might be able to exploit. Is this enough? No. Why not? Because modern software development includes software that is composed from different open source components. To be certain our code is secure, we cannot simply analyze all of our own source code, we must have confidence that third-party components are secure as well.

This is true for every aspect of metadata. For example, we can test our code for performance. We can use benchmarking tools and application performance management (APM) systems to discover if a component we've just written is performing well enough to go to production. Is that enough? Once again, the answer is no. We need to know about the performance of *all* the components we use – those coming from other teams in our organizations, as well as those coming from third-party sources.

The same type of thinking applies when it comes to licenses or any other aspect of the architecture of the software we produce and distribute. And we need to be mindful of how quickly things can and will shift in the world of software development. For instance, at one moment in time, we might incorporate a particular company's third-party libraries as a login component. Just because that company's product is good today doesn't mean it will be good tomorrow. Perhaps a new CVE about a fatal security flaw will be discovered; perhaps the provider won't be able to keep up with the pace of innovation; or perhaps some competitor will come out with a product that's better. And maybe we'll decide to switch to another provider, only to discover later that our original provider has made improvements sufficient for us to switch back. If we're reliant on third-party solutions, we need to be paying attention, and making decisions accordingly.

"Your Data Security is Important to Us"

At present, if we want to check whether an artifact is vulnerable, we can rely on a number of good informational resources. One that is particularly helpful is the National Vulnerability Database (NVD), a service of the Information Technology Laboratory (ITL), operated by the U.S. National Institute of Standards and Technology (NIST). However, as of yet, there is no single repository of information that can address all of the questions we might have about all software components.

Regardless of which database we might use, we have a more fundamental question: How is a given artifact to be identified in any particular database? If there are no standards, how can we know if an inquiry we submit has been conclusively answered? A mistake here can impact the data security of millions of people. This might be what happened in 2017 to the consumer credit reporting agency, Equifax. A data breach occurred that exposed the sensitive private information (names, dates of birth, social security numbers, etc.) of over 145 million U.S. consumers. It also resulted in over 200,000 credit card numbers being illegally accessed.

So, what happened?

Equifax had built a container to store all of the personal identifying information (PII) of its customers. The company used a third-party resource to do this – *Apache Struts 2* – a free, open source, and (as it turned out) quite vulnerable Java library. The firm wasn't necessarily wrong to use Struts 2. After all, it had been embraced by the software industry for almost a decade. A significant majority of websites written in Java had been using Struts, making it a de facto standard during that period.

By early 2017, however, Struts 2 was no longer the best available web framework in the marketplace. It had become a legacy resource and was on its way out, not least because it had racked up a history of security vulnerabilities. According to the Common Vulnerability Scoring System (CVSS), since the debut of Apache Struts 2 in 2007, fourteen of its vulnerabilities had rated hair-on-fire scores of 9 or above (on a scale of 10). Apache released a patch for the fifteenth such vulnerability – which had achieved the dubious distinction of a "perfect" CVSS 10-score – in March 2017. Disastrously, Equifax wasn't paying attention. Two months went by and the company still hadn't applied the patch. By May 2017, Equifax was so vulnerable that the breach it suffered was the cyberattack equivalent of punching a fist through a decorative Japanese room divider. Data flowed out of its systems over the course of several weeks, ultimately costing the company and its insurers hundreds of millions of dollars. In the aftermath of the fiasco, firms that had still been using Struts 2 abandoned it in droves.

Universalizing Metadata

Much has been written and said about what happened at Equifax. But is it a given that a simple dose of due diligence will always be the perfect path to avoiding catastrophe? Let's say that right now we want to determine the current vulnerability status of Struts 2. We could visit the National Vulnerabilities Database. How should we search for it there? Should we enter its name as *Struts 2*, *struts2*, or *Apache Struts 2*? Should we enter its SHA1 checksum, it's GAV coordinates (org.apache.struts:struts2-core), or should we use some other type of identifier? What if we don't find anything on the NVD? How should we carry out a search in another database?

Is there any way to perform a crosscheck? Maybe it's registered with some databases and not others.

So we have several big problems. First, when we want to perform a search, there's no place for "one-stop shopping." Second, regardless of where we go, the data we're seeking might not be available. Third, if the data is available, there's no uniform methodology for querying the components we're using. But with so much metadata being generated from so many different sources, we might begin to think that this is all getting to be a bit too complicated. It is. That's why, as part of the liquid software revolution, it will be wise to standardize the methodologies through which metadata is generated, transferred, and read.

We understand that many in the software industry react to the idea of standardization with trepidation, because past attempts at developing standards have not been very successful. This is not because there are serious disagreements about the benefits of establishing standards. And it certainly isn't because the industry lacks the talent or inventiveness to create useful standards. It's that in too many instances, even where consensus has existed that standardization would be helpful, when a dozen different entities created the needed "standard," instead of simplifying the situation, things only became more complex.

The Solution: A Metadata Scribe

In late 2017, an open source initiative called *Grafeas* (the Greek word for "scribe") was launched, its objective being to "define a uniform way for auditing and governing the modern software supply chain." Grafeas would like to gather metadata about everything through the implementation of an industry-accepted common model for sharing metadata about software artifacts and releases. The concept envisions acquiring and pooling metadata from both internal and external sources, in order to construct a more complete picture about components in circulation and use.

In practical application, NVD can expose this data in Grafeas format, which renders it universally understandable, particularly to machine-driven platforms and systems. Metadata can be tagged with a mutually agreed upon identifier, such as a checksum of an artifact, which can then be compared with all known checksums and all known vulnerabilities. Thereafter, Grafeas can provide a response in the form of an adjacent file that can flow through continuous update pipelines. A given file might indicate that we have encountered instances of particular vulnerabilities. In an automated system, this would trigger a block, which would prevent the problematic artifact from being further promoted in a production or distribution pipeline.

While this central database of vulnerabilities is the most obvious example of what Grafeas can do, the possibilities are enormous. For example, when handling metadata that's internal to a company, we will typically see separate divisions and different teams sharing metadata. But let's say that one particular firm is using a component that is completely internal, and the outside world doesn't know it exists. Under normal circumstances, this component would never appear in any external database. However, through the use of a Grafeas-compatible source code security analyzer, we might be able to detect a pattern in that component's code that could present a security vulnerability. Again, Grafeas can provide a response in the form of a metadata file that streams this information inside an organization. Then, whenever an automatic pipeline needs to vet artifacts for security breaches, it will receive a uniformly formatted document, with the same exact metadata from the outside database and the inside source. This will help it to ban artifacts, as appropriate, whether they're based on Struts 2 or an internal component that's just been revealed to contain some suspicious looking source code.

The Grafeas initiative is encouraging a dramatic increase in the production and use of metadata. As we have said several times, metadata is the key to continuous update success. Metadata should be registered for every action we take in development and should be consulted in every decision that needs to be made in production and promotion. We should produce metadata at every phase of continuous integration, starting from the build server. We should log information regarding how a particular artifact was built, who initiated the build, what the environment variables were, which versions of system dependencies were used, how long the build took, and so forth. Following this, we want metadata regarding QA. For example, as we perform unit tests, we should register whether our artifacts have passed or not, and whether the tests triggered any concerns or warnings. The same should hold true for recording integration test metadata, as we will want information to verify stability or alert us about instabilities. We should gather and register metadata equally about every test we perform. Since we cannot be certain about the future and what information we might need – let alone information that can help us avoid a calamity – the gathering of copious amounts of metadata should become routine across the industry.

A World in Which Grafeas Data is Everywhere

Grafeas is unique in that it acknowledges a reality in today's software industry – the existence of complicated use cases, where software includes components from internal *and* external sources. Grafeas is designed to be able to mix and match the metadata arising from both. Depending on the nature of what we're building, we might integrate information from various components that we're using. In such situations, external metadata can become part of our internal metadata. Conversely, we might have internal metadata published in in-house databases. If we begin to work on an open source library, we might want to disclose our internal metadata to public metadata sources, so others could benefit from this information.

With increasing amounts of metadata, we will create opportunities to check and recheck our components before they are deployed to runtime servers. One example of this is an initiative called *Kritis* (Greek for "judge"), a rule engine for *Kubernetes* that operates on Grafeas metadata. This tool will allow us to write rules to direct the execution of a final pre-deployment check. If the check encounters any security vulnerabilities, the rule will direct the system not to move forward to deployment.

The Kritis project is an acknowledgement of another reality of modern software, which is that components that have already been tested as stable and secure today aren't guaranteed to remain in that state tomorrow. We might have a component that's been in production for two years, and then suddenly discover there are vulnerabilities in every layer of our dependencies. Obviously, this would require us to take action on artifacts that are already in production. We want the software industry to evolve to the point where liquid software is automatically pinging Grafeas-enabled metadata databases at regular intervals (say, every 24 hours or less) to make sure that something we've verified at one point in time is still secure a bit further down the line.

The Grafeas metadata description initiative seeks to establish universality in the way we register queries about components, and to standardize the format of responses returned from those queries. It's important to note, however, that any tools using this format must be adjusted individually by the companies that produce them. Grafeas doesn't maintain any centralized service, nor does the project intend to acquire and centralize existing databases.

If Grafeas is successful, it might well become an integral and indispensable part of the liquid software revolution. This would certainly be the case if, eventually, continuous update pipelines can issue standardized Grafeas requests to the NVD and other vulnerability databases, and receive standardized Grafeas responses that can be parsed automatically. Under such a scenario, decision-making regarding whether we want our artifacts to proceed in a given pipeline or not would become decentralized, and therefore much simpler and more secure.

CHAPTER 2: WHERE WE'VE BEEN

"Disruptors don't have to discover something new;
they just have to discover
a practical use for new discoveries."
– Jay Samit, digital media innovator

How We Got Here

There have been three great innovations in human history – language, money, and software. Fundamentally, all of them deal with information and enable significant exchanges of value between vast groups of people. Their collective impact is incalculable.

We all understand the importance and impact of words. We, the authors of this book, are communicating ideas, and you, the reader, are absorbing (perhaps even grappling with) them because of our shared ability to transmit and grasp utterances, thoughts, and concepts via the vehicle of language.

Money allows us to assign relative and changeable values to goods and services. It creates opportunities for us to offer tangible gifts and rewards, as well as loans that make it possible for others to secure advantages otherwise unobtainable with their own resources. It also establishes the freedom to create and increase wealth through activities ranging from sensible investing to high stakes gambling. From rare seashells and metal coins to crypto 1s and 0s, currency has been a fact of everyday life for thousands of years, and likely will be for all time to come.

Imagine that we had a time machine and could actually witness the dawn of language and the dawn of money with our own eyes, and observe their development across the millennia. Mind-blowing as that would be, we'd be observing gradual, incremental, often infinitesimal changes over enormous swaths of time and circumstance.

Now, consider humanity's third great innovation – software. It still has a couple of decades to go before it can celebrate its centenary! Over the course of a mere eighty years, its power, consequences, and repercussions on our planet have been astonishing. Although language, money, and software are not directly comparable, the evolution of the highly complex and deeply stratified ways in which the first two have come to be used took centuries upon centuries. Software, on the other hand, matured at lightning speed. It would be as if human language had begun 100,000 years ago and just a week later, the works of Shakespeare had been produced; as if the first exchanges of carved stones had occurred when it did and, a year later, the World Bank had come into being!

The smartphones we carry around pack more computing power than the Saturn V rocket systems that took men to the moon. Software is woven into the daily fabric of our lives – from portable devices and desktop office suites to ATM machines, airport check-in kiosks, and those fancy new machines at the local fast food joint on which you can order your next burger and fries. In addition to all of that, software is operating in the background almost everywhere. We do not directly interact with this software, yet it runs incalculable numbers of systems, and maintains much of the infrastructure of modern society. With every passing day, software is more of who we are and what we do. All by itself, the Internet of Things – that exploding universe of common use items that are software-controlled and network-connected – is radically changing not only how we use those things; it's changing our expectations of their capabilities, and our expectations of life in general.

Software is our contemporary history, and its most breathtaking advancements are happening right now!

In the beginning, software and hardware were essentially one. It all began in 1948, when a stored-program computer first ran a piece of software. Within a decade, an industry had arisen that served private businesses and government institutions with electronic computing power. At this point, the "acquisition of software" as yet had no independent meaning. A machine would be purchased from what we now call an Original Equipment Manufacturers (OEM), and it came with its own software, engineered and installed by the manufacturer.

By the mid-1960s, computers were fast evolving from useful to indispensable tools. Demand for the machines increased, and parallel demands arose for those machines to perform more complex tasks – and for these tasks to reliably be executed in decreasing amounts of time. It was during this period that Gordon Moore observed a truth whose impact on the computer industry could not have been greater if he had chiseled it into a stone tablet and handed it down from a mountain. Later known as Moore's Law, it asserted that the number of components that could be accommodated in a dense, integrated circuit would double approximately every two years. This turned out to be a remarkably accurate assessment, not merely of what Moore saw occurring, but also of what was to come during the half-century that followed. That is, the exponential advancement in raw computing power of hardware as, at the same time, that hardware became ever more compact.

In 2015, Intel CEO Brian Krzanich stated it in an even more awe-inspiring fashion. He took as his basis of measurement a 1971 Volkswagen Beetle and applied the basic concepts of Moore's Law to that vehicle. His extrapolation led to his assertion that 34 years of progress would have resulted in a car in which you could travel 300,000 miles per hour, go two million miles on a single gallon of gas, and at a cost of less than five cents.

By the early 1980s, an environmental transformation got underway, as software started to be decoupled from hardware and became an individual entity sold on its own. As a result, a small handful of large corporate computer giants could no longer harness all of the creativity and imagination that demand was inspiring. But even as software was emerging as a discrete product, much of the industry was still dominated by relatively monolithic packages for which organizations were paying. A significant amount of the functionalities contained within those software bundles often went unutilized by those organizations.

Writing software was a time-consuming and personnel-intensive process. From the early 1980s onward, high profile creators such as Apple, Microsoft, and Oracle released major upgrades to their operating systems and applications at significant ribbon-cutting events approximately every two years. The concept (and sale) of software versions became mainstream.

A huge amount of concentrated energy goes into making, testing, and verifying versions to make them as good as they can be before introducing them to the marketplace. Once a version is released, changes and fixes to errors or bugs require a burdensome process of patching. Depending on the severity of any particular problem, end-users may experience these repair processes in the form of costly delays in deployment, time-consuming workarounds, and periodic downtimes after implementation.

The main issue with this process is the sheer quantity of software that's being produced. This quantity is necessarily consequential to quality, because the design of software and quality control systems is generally geared toward big picture, not granular, impacts. Software creators usually develop monolithic packages within the confines of their own companies. The process doesn't allow them to be and *continually remain* in contact with their users. For the most part, versions are created, and tests are performed, within the closed loop of the individual software company. Even the most inventive minds and the best research are not substitutes for feedback from real-world environments that allow software firms to discover where problems exist and what needs fixing. In the major release context, acquiring that information from users, adequately addressing issues and concerns, and then releasing updates, all comprise a significant process that may take an entire year, if not longer, to complete.

Simply put, while each new version of a software package has almost always been meant to herald the introduction of a significant improvement, things haven't always turned out the way they were intended. There are infamous examples of new version upgrades of existing and well-established software packages that were released only to become spectacular flops. *Microsoft Vista* is just one example. Even where new versions have been successful, users had to become accustomed to the idea that these products would require periodic updates to patch security issues and fix bugs. For this reason, many users, particularly users of major operating systems – whether simple end-users or software industry professionals – have become wary of upgrades. Some updates are relatively small and easy to acquire and apply, while others are delivered by way of bundled service packs, making them seem like the equivalent to upgrade installations. Often, users will choose to wait a year or more after an upgrade release before moving to a new version.

Large or small, one thing has remained constant; while people may be interested in the value that new features of an upgrade provide, most of them have no idea, nor much interest in, what is contained in patches. As far as most end-users are concerned, they have purchased a product intended to facilitate business productivity, make their lives easier, offer more entertainment options, and so forth. And they simply want that product to work.

Furthermore, the overwhelming majority of users don't know, nor do they care to know, the version number of the software they are using. While most probably have some understanding of the need to operate computing devices in a secure manner, they don't want to have to monitor whether a particular piece of software is properly up to date. In a perfect software user's world, whatever needs to happen in order for them to receive, install, and start using an update will occur transparently, in the background – with no need for them to do anything at all!

Certainly, there have been improvements toward this end. Most computer users can select to have the majority of their software updates automatically downloaded and installed. Indeed, users of smartphones, tablets, and other newer digital devices routinely adjust their settings to auto-install app updates. Software engineers and DevOps personnel can also opt for automatic runtime updates. This is progress, to be sure, but there are still inconsistencies in this realm.

While much can now be automated, user intervention is still required, periodically, for certain updates. User participation in the process may be as simple as approving the installation of an update. However, the vast majority of users have no clue as to the purpose or content of the updates they receive, or why their approval is necessary. Users can be left with the feeling that they are being asked to make a decision about implementing something that the software company itself is eminently more qualified to execute without user involvement. The more cynically minded might suggest there's little or no reason for users to be asked to approve updates other than to release vendors from any liability. User approvals are typically associated with lengthy and complicated legal documents that are rarely read, and clicking assent to an update usually means agreeing to hold that vendor blameless for any resultant harm to one's hardware, other software, or personal files.

Businesses and managers have long sought opportunities to increase productivity by accomplishing tasks with greater speed and efficiency. And, for too long, employees and software engineers alike have reported that they are more capable of achieving their goals on their personally owned computers than at their office workstations. Usually this was due entirely to the comparative ease and speed with which consumer software could be updated versus the slower and more cumbersome processes needed to update enterprise systems. The fact that millions have experienced better computing at home than in the workplace has helped to propel significant improvements in enterprise software.

Consumers are increasingly of the mindset that they would like to purchase or acquire software that they take ownership of and use for purpose-specific objectives. They don't want unnecessary stuff! This has impacted software development such that significant thought and action has gone into the breaking up of software suites into smaller modules. Software is now being sold in more discrete, function-specific units. From a technical angle, this has manifested in the rise of serverless and microservice architectures, which constitute a more efficient and streamlined approach to software development and updating, offering very specific services and allowing for greater attention to detail. Modules interact with one another via an equally simple approach to the development of a services interface.

When the Going Gets Tough, the Tough Git Going

Linus Torvalds, the Finnish-American software engineer and open source pioneer who designed the *Linux* kernel, also created (perhaps even more notably) *Git*. When introduced in 2005, Git was a more comprehensive – and more comprehensively flexible – version control system than the software world had yet seen. Git can coordinate the work executed by everyone working on a computer file, and it can track all changes made to that file. While it can perform this service on any computer file, the software development has primarily used Git community as a speedy and efficient means of source code management.

Necessity was certainly the mother of the Git invention. Pre-Git, most Linux developers were using a proprietary source control management (SCM) system, *BitKeeper*. When its copyright holder halted free access to the system in 2005, Torvalds saw it as perfectly logical for the open source Linux community to be supported by an open source version control system capable of assuring data integrity across distributed, non-linear workflows.

Git is similar to BitKeeper and many other distributed version control systems in that each and every Git directory on every computer on which it resides is a comprehensive historical repository of all actions taken on a particular file. It offers full version tracking functionalities and the ability to operate independent of a network or centralized server.

In creating Git, Torvalds considered the spectrum of client-server version control systems then available, which in addition to BitKeeper included Concurrent Versions System (CVS) and Subversion (SVN). Torvalds noted that Subversion's creators were especially proud of its branching functionality, which he considered a sort of half-measure, since it was his conviction that branching is useless if branches cannot subsequently be merged. He said that SVN "...talks very loudly about how they do CVS right by making branching really cheap" and can make this happen exceedingly quickly. But he asserted that even if branching "takes a millionth of a second to do," that's not the problem. The issue is merging. Torvalds said "branches are completely useless unless you merge them, and SVN cannot merge anything at all. You can merge things once, but because SVN then forgets what you did, you can never ever merge anything again without getting horrible, horrible conflicts."

Git therefore sought not only to address the tracking of discrete changes in workflows, but also when and how merges take place. It was revolutionary in recognizing a fundamental issue that needed solving. It was also an acknowledgement that as the software world evolved and more people became involved in projects in increasingly decentralized settings – more branching and more merging would result. Git embraced this reality. It surpassed Subversion in a quantum leap forward, allowing a vast increase in the number of branching and merging operations that could be executed.

OSGi and What Might Have Been: An Instructive Tale

Java, with its Java Virtual Machine (JVM) and dynamic class loader, was the first big successful platform available for the development and deployment of modular software programs and libraries. The Open Services Gateway initiative (OSGi), now the OSGi Alliance, was founded in 1999 as a means of capitalizing on the capability of the JVM to accommodate continuous updates of small packages and components running on it. At the runtime level, the JVM has allowed us to direct calls from an old version to a new version, and to dynamically and rapidly recreate the graph of dependencies of those packages. In fact, practically all of the fundamental concepts of liquid software, including how to reconnect an API, how to handle dependencies, and how to transparently update a system, were parts of the mission of the OSGi. The initiative was focused only on the Java platform and the JVM, which were extremely successful during the early years after the turn of the century. As of this writing, the JVM is still running the majority of the world's websites.

Nevertheless, OSGi has fallen into significant decline. We believe this happened because they never gave due consideration to developers. As a result, the developers of continuously updateable Java Archives (JARs) and automatically updateable JAR components were left with a lot of extra work to do. In the beginning, many developers and companies felt the additional effort was worth it. As time went by, the effort and expense required to create an OSGi JAR became less cost-beneficial, particularly as the cost of creating new VMs continually trended downward. Contributing to this was the availability of alternatives such as VMware and, later, Docker.

There was a push to try to design tools to facilitate the creation of OSGi JAR components, but these were developer innovations and not part of the runtime platform. Eventually, the tooling became too complex and tedious, and the whole process generated a lot of friction between the tooling and the runtime platform. As the platform continued to evolve, the more the effort to create developer tools intensified. Like trains running on parallel tracks, they might have been going in the same direction, but that didn't necessarily mean they'd arrive at the same station.

In the end, it came down to a mathematical proof, which revealed some very fundamental flaws in the way OSGi handled dependency declarations. It was objectively demonstrated that there were many times and situations in which it was mathematically impossible to update the JAR components running on the JVM and move forward. Huge amounts of computational time and power went into finding the few solutions that could be found. It was frustrating, inefficient, costly...and silly!

The way the OSGi platform was updating JARs became a kind of black box. To be certain that all the component parts were functioning correctly, developers would go to the trouble of testing everything. This would be followed by a lot of heavy tooling to create the packages, which were deployed to complicated platforms only to find out that the whole effort was a bust! Worse, the developers had no idea why! There were so many hurdles to overcome along the way – so many things happening between what was declared during the tooling process (which was *supposed* to make life easier) and what was running on the platform – that developers had no way to actually identify the source of a problem.

What's happening when a continuous update is being executed needs to be transparent to developers. In the case of the OSGi platform, history might have been quite different had the developer experience been taken into account right from the start, and had been an integral (as opposed to peripheral) part of its planning and development.

The Rise of the Machines

To make continuous updates the norm, DevOps – and the wider software industry – must embrace the rise of the machines. At present, there are enormous inefficiencies and bottlenecks baked into our software development systems. We have legions of people doing the same tasks over and over again – tasks that can be automated and handled more rapidly, productively, and economically by computers. Several large companies have already moved in this direction. The fact that they have done so should serve as a herald to everyone else in the industry. While current examples are not necessarily replicable (due to the use of proprietary systems), they are nevertheless instructive.

Similar to Newton's First Law of Motion (a body at rest will tend to remain at rest unless acted upon by an outside force), when certain systems are in place, individuals become accustomed to doing things in a particular way, and they tend to continue along that same path. Bluntly stated: People dislike change and often resist it.

Resistance is sometimes driven by anxieties about time and productivity. After all, most of us are busy enough just getting our job done in the manner to which we've become accustomed. Change generally requires that we slow down, or even stop what we're currently doing, to consider how things might be done differently. If we discover a better way, additional time and energy must be devoted to devising and implementing new procedures, adopting new tools, and maybe even reorienting our entire way of working.

Nevertheless, there is now an exponential demand for software and a rising desire for interconnectivity and interactivity between devices and across platforms. Software firms must invest the necessary capital and effort to be a part of the liquid software revolution. Fundamental business logic makes this strategically consequential. Making the changes necessary to deliver continuous updates will, in the end, optimize the operations of *all* software companies. It will also allow developers to concentrate their talents where they will be of maximum service (i.e., in the creation of highly-targeted solutions for end users). In so doing, all software creators will increase their opportunities to win over and retain customers, which will bring positive bottom line results. With the right tools in place, automation significantly reduces waste, and the effects are multiplied when automated systems serve software operating in a cloud-based environment.

From a cost per CPU hour standpoint, the cost of a machine is dramatically less than the cost of an engineer. For example, currently, the marginal cost of per hour machine operations for Amazon Web Services (AWS) is diminishing toward $0.02, whereas the cost for a good engineer is between $100-200. That makes it four orders of magnitude cheaper for Amazon to run an automation once it's written.

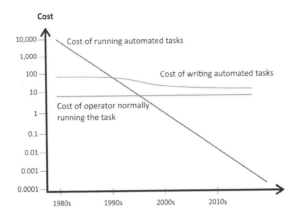

Automation's Relative Costs Over Time

Curiously, the industry didn't start out like this. In the early days of software development, a CPU hour on a mainframe computer was about one hundred times more expensive than the cost of an engineer. Despite how profoundly times have changed, the software industry has yet to fully grasp the implications of such progress. There is still far too much human involvement, and too many needless processes involved in producing software. There remain far too many managers who continue to believe that devoting personnel hours to setting CPU time, memory, and disk parameters is an optimal way to save money. This is particularly ironic considering the fact that for many years now, the mantra, "People are expensive, computers are free" has circulated widely among software professionals.

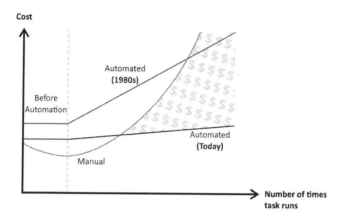

The ROI of Automation

With this said, we want to be clear. The argument here is not for machines that will address exactly the same needs, operate in exactly the same environments, and do exactly the same jobs over and over again. Wasting machine and CPU cycle time is not the way to go. What we want is efficient, binary-driven development.

Taking Queues from the Auto Industry

Like the construction of cars at the dawn of the automotive age, software used to be written from bottom to top, originating from low-level assembly code. It was basically some people creating software from scratch in their basements or garages. If any of the first manufactured cars had a problem, they would have to go back to where they were created; the builders were the only ones capable of making repairs. There were no ancillary industries, such as parts suppliers and fix-it shops. There was also nothing like what we would now call "quality control". The materials, parts, components, and processes that were produced by the manufacturers were the be-all and end-all of the nascent automotive industry. Software was created and maintained in a very similar fashion.

When Henry Ford came along with a very significant innovation – the assembly line – no longer were cars the product of automotive artisans. Now they could be assembled with standardized parts – designed and tested to achieve certain established levels of quality and endurance. Construction of automobiles became a series of specialized and discrete tasks executed by assembly line workers. All of this individualization and automation vastly increased car production while decreasing manufacturing costs, which in turn lowered prices to consumers and dramatically increased access to automobiles by average citizens.

Software engineering, manufacture, distribution, and support have evolved as well. Process has become increasingly automated and industrialized. The auto industry analogy is not a perfect one, though. For a variety of reasons, software production has never achieved complete industrialization. Software factories where all processes – start to finish – are executed under a single roof have never really succeeded. This may be because there is still a misalignment between the world of DevOps and the broader software industry it supports.

The most modern incarnation of the automotive manufacturing experience is where we may see a further extension of our analogy. We have robotic assembly lines, where machines – not people – are carrying out very precise construction tasks. These robots are capable of producing levels of precision, consistency, and quality that are nearly impossible for humans to replicate, and they are certainly able to produce far greater quantities of output.

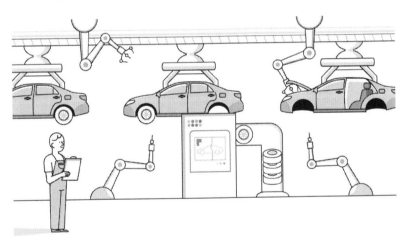

We can think of continuous deployment as being similar to the full automation of the production of factory-built cars, where all processes related to the assembly of those vehicles (from parts production to QA testing) are handled by machines. The vehicle that is "deployed" to the customer is the end product of all those automated processes. The paradigm shift to continuous updates would be somewhat akin to the glove compartment of every vehicle containing a little robot that could execute modifications, adaptations, and repairs on a continuous basis.

The mass manufacture of modern motor vehicles is, of course, not a single, self-contained set of processes taking place in one building along a dedicated assembly line. In fact, numerous companies in far-flung locales execute diverse procedures. These companies are designing, producing, testing, and quality-certifying parts and components that will be integrated into an end product. All of these companies, including the one responsible for final assembly of the vehicles, are reliant on robots for many manufacturing tasks. The robots are programmed to carry out an enormous range of functions, relieving human beings of many of the repetitive, mundane operations that go into the construction of the product. QA engineers don't work directly with the vehicles, but rather with the machines that deal with their manufacture. DevOps engineers don't concentrate on the actual production of the cars, but rather, on the robots that are managing, maintaining, monitoring, and logging the automobiles on the assembly line. When the marketplace rewards a well-designed, well-manufactured car through its purchases, it is tacitly endorsing all of those responsible and everything that went into that vehicle. With ever increasing automation in all of these companies, human attention is directly focused on the machines and the software running their systems. The result – and this is no different than what we see in so many aspects of our lives currently – greater demands are being placed on software to operate and maintain systems in a smart manner.

The automotive industry, like so many other modern industries, automates manufacturing and other processes to achieve efficiencies that allow them to sell better products at attractive prices. As companies strive toward greater innovation, they expect the software running their systems to be ever more responsive and intuitive.

There is, however, a distance yet to be traveled. The liquid software revolution demands that software developers *commit* to automating the processes that will bridge the gap between continuous deployment and continuous updates. This will liberate DevOps personnel from tasks that machines are eminently capable of carrying out, and they will spend more time and creativity on new and improved functionalities.

The further industrialization of software production – especially the writing of code – will be experienced by end-users silently, transparently, and seamlessly, as software receives steady streams of continuous updates. To set this flow in motion we must have software capable of writing software, and of executing updates on any platform, within any system, and in any environment.

Change (of Mind) Takes Time

For the liquid software revolution to truly succeed, user mindsets need to change. In many ways, this is at the heart of what needs to be fixed. This issue is somewhat similar to that of data backups. People were reminded for years to back up their personal data. It was something they had to do, and they had to remember to do it on a regular basis. Eventually, a variety of data backup systems and services arose that facilitated the process. The best of these allowed for set-it-and-forget-it operations. This was an improvement, although data retrieval and recovery were not always simple or seamless. Then, along came the cloud, with some systems backing up our data in real time, with anywhere-any-moment access just a few clicks away.

There's absolutely nothing surprising about this progression. Like so many things that are good for us, and that we know we should do, taking the proactive steps to do those things often gets left for "tomorrow". If those things were quick and easy, we'd do them. We frequently don't because they're inconvenient, annoying, or even painful. We're relieved and often thrilled when someone else figures out a way to handle those things for us and we don't have to get involved at all.

Substantive advances have already been made to make operating system updates and upgrades relatively swift and efficient. The Debian Project introduced – and RedHat later copied – an effective approach to delivering automatic operating system updates. The Linux world managed these types of updates for years before Apple began doing the same, while Microsoft has yet to enter the playing field. Doing things right means dedicating time, effort, and resources to making sure that updates arrive fully ready. Careful attention must be paid to pre-processing, ensuring that all data will be capable of being migrated correctly. Users must have confidence that everything will proceed in an uneventful fashion. They need to be assured that just as soon as an update process completes, a thoroughly up-to-date computer or device is just a restart away.

An internet search for the terms "iOS" or "Android" and "automatic updates" reveals many results centered around the theme, "How do I turn it off?!" People are conspicuously confused and exasperated by the way most updates are currently executed. They would prefer automatic, transparent, and secure updates — a goal whose full achievement will require a little more time and quite a bit of work.

The work already done in some environments, gave us information on not only what needs to be done, but on how to do it. We learned, for example, that no amount of reminders will ever make manual data backups the norm. We reached the conclusion that technologies, such as the cloud, needed to evolve to create the automated means by which users can regularly and continually back up their data. These days, automatic backups to the cloud are practically a default process of digital devices that produce personal or business data.

As with data backups, the rest of the software industry is making progress in evolutionary steps. Pressure from customers for continuous updates is steadily building, but hasn't reached critical mass yet. Development costs for most software development organizations are dropping dramatically. It's now possible to update a complete software stack on one's own runtime and in one's own environment, and to make ready-to-use updates transparent and nuisance free. Liquid software is possible now, and we believe that continuous updates will eventually become just another default process. We hope this book will serve as your encouragement and inspiration to become a liquid software revolutionary! We hope you will lead the charge to make this a reality in your corner of the software industry.

 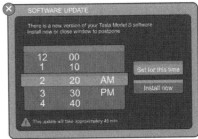

The Impact of Forced Updates

Revving Up the Machines

While Git has dramatically improved the branching and merging of files, we are still very much living in a world where software version deployments occur through the creation of large runtime-ready files (e.g., machine images, containers, executables) and the manual use of other tools. This is a barrier to continuous updating.

Granted, several innovations have emerged in recent years that are squarely focused on automating file creation and removing many manual processes, which helps to accelerate deployments. Most notable among these is Docker. Even these new approaches have their limits, however, as continuous deployments can be limited to software size and complexity threshold values. Continuous updating seeks to create an environment where such boundary limitations no longer exist. When this becomes possible, the opportunities to update more software more often will rise exponentially.

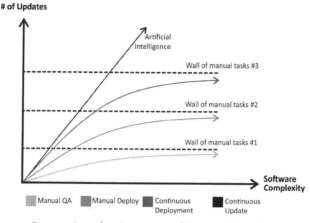

Removing the Barriers of Manual Tasks

For updates to be truly continuous, all processes (building, validating, and deploying) must be automated and secure. All processes must be executable on a range of runtimes. New deployments must take place with active data and active users on running systems. This is the difference between continuous deployments and continuous updates. And it explicitly means that particular care and attention must be paid to the detection and resolution of issues related to serious bugs. These are the liquid software revolution's most pressing challenges.

CHAPTER 3:
WHERE WE ARE AND
WHAT'S WRONG WITH IT

*"Meaningful innovation does not need to be based on
outright invention. Rather, there is an exhilarating shortcut.
It is based on bold, new combinations of already existing
components that simultaneously unlock heightened levels
of consumer value and reduce costs."*
– Gabor George Burt, innovation expert

Release Fast or Die

Shortened release cycles with reduced batch sizes are a hallmark of the liquid software revolution of continuous updates. Through the use of machines, liquid software will diminish complexity by breaking down software into small pieces. This will result in an increase in variables and interactions, and, therefore, an increase in problems requiring attention. However, small pieces will allow for more focused and nimble management, as well as more rapid execution of patches and updates.

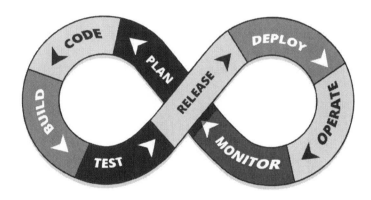

The Infinite Cycle of DevOps

Cycle time is a critical metric. It is a measurement of the total span of time it takes for a process to run, start to finish. An example of this is the length of time that elapses between the origination of a new idea for a software feature and the moment the governing version control system receives a commit of the new feature's changes to the source code repository.

Anyone involved in DevOps should see decreased cycle times (that still produce high quality outputs at lower cost) as a desirable goal, because this will:

- reduce the time between bug or vulnerability detections and their fixes being released

- accelerate the delivery of new and improved features

- stimulate progress toward the establishment of self-operating rapid improvement processes that are stable, secure and reliable

- enhance capacity, as flow optimization will enable an increased number of changes to be produced within shorter periods of time

- reduce lead times, inventories, backlogs, and bottlenecks, as flow optimization will improve the management of concurrent projects in process, and

- increase profits

Pressures to secure these advances are profoundly driven by the mobile device marketplace and the exploding universe of IoT products. With so many items being branded as "smart", that characteristic is no longer a novelty; it's the norm. We assume that smart features will be standard, and we expect all manner of electronic items to be not just increasingly interactive, but intuitive as well.

The IoT market is already huge. Just a few years ago, momentum trends were suggesting that by 2020 our planet would be home to tens of billions of devices connected to the internet. Of course, that prediction was before the consumer marketplace introduction of a whole range of new products, including smart speakers equipped with virtual assistants, such as Amazon's *Alexa* and *Google Assistant*. It's now a safe bet that even "tens of billions" is a low estimate.

In the realm of IoT, continuous updates will be updating software on runtimes that neither individuals nor companies will control or own. Users will simply operate the functionalities being offered by the software that is running on their devices. This is a last-mile advancement over continuous deployment – a process where deployments are pushed out to locally controlled data centers and production systems, which impact locally controlled runtimes. Those overseeing the local control generally know the runtimes to which deployments are being made. Continuous updates via liquid software expand the magnitude and speed of what can happen. They change the paradigm, because continuous update runtimes are those where local control has no impact on that which is being pushed out, nor are they an intervention option to selectively pull updates in.

The thin line between target environment and product disappears when we consider IoT products such as intelligent toothbrushes, connected clothing, automotive systems, smart home thermostats, door locks, and lighting arrays. In these instances, the productive operational environment is the product itself. Once again, technical details are irrelevant to the user. What matters is the delivery of a great user experience. These products are ideally suited for continuous updates. Their utility in the moment and their competitive viability in the marketplace will increasingly depend on their ability to incorporate rolled out changes very quickly. The more quickly changes are deployed, the fewer malfunctions and failures there will be. This, in turn, will raise user confidence and brand loyalty. Product manufacturers will be rewarded for delivering smooth operations and seamless services that liberate their customers from technical concerns.

The liquid software revolution is in progress, and it has battles yet to be fought and won. Smart companies making smart products understand that they will be best served by liquid software, because continuous updating assures a marketplace edge.

Continuous updating will inspire confidence only when robust security mechanisms are in place that confirm the safety of the software being streamed to systems and devices. As well, the quality of the software updates must improve, particularly to reassure customers that critical systems are not being exposed to exploitable vulnerabilities. There must also be a way for automatic updates to be coordinated with the systems they are updating, in order to verify full compatibility. This means establishing the manner by which continuous updates (and all the systems involved in creating, testing, and maintaining them) can flow to any platform and communicate across platforms seamlessly.

If They Can Send a Man to the Moon, Why Can't They...

In terms of software, we've already taken a giant leap for mankind. We've updated systems aboard capsules en route to the moon, and we've updated spacecraft on Mars. We now update all manner of systems continuously, and doing so is on the increase. When we refresh a webpage in a browser, we're likely encountering updated software. Storage solutions (even low-level solutions) need updates for their controllers and drivers, and for management and storage of bytes on disks. This is occurring in countless infrastructure environments out of absolute necessity, as few can afford the time, and many don't even have the ability, to shut down their storage technologies. They'd love to receive on-the-fly, over-the-air updates with zero downtime. And once they really experience the benefits, doubtless they'll soon *demand* continuous updates.

We can do this *and* send human beings to the moon! So, it's not inability to make continuous updates the norm that's holding us back – it's laziness.

That's not to be glib about the matter, as we recognize that making this transition is a technical challenge, and in many firms also a corporate culture challenge. These are new ways of doing things. These are things that need to be taught, tested, and developed. It means dealing with API routing and transitions, transparent schema changes, method calls, and many related issues. And all this adds expense. It adds time. In the long run, however, particularly if this is where the trends are leading, the cost-benefits of moving in this direction will be evident.

As of this writing, the world is still updating whole systems – product-by-product, app-by-app, and feature-by-feature – with no running data at the time of the updates. And a large segment of the developer community still holds the attitude: "Let's not worry about this now. No harm done in sticking with what we know. It's not a big deal to ask users to shut down their systems and reboot two or three times to acquire a new feature." The problem with this thinking is that these developers aren't giving due consideration to all those users who have opted to turn off their updates. By not sensibly assessing human nature and the most basic of user preferences, this don't-worry-it's-not-a-big-deal attitude is actually doing harm. If users aren't accepting updates because they don't want to deal with interruptions and even minimal hassles, then all the good work being done to improve software isn't reaching as many users as possible. This can impact company sales and reputations. Worse, this can affect security when users are not receiving necessary patches to resolve breaches and other security flaws.

Of course, it's not only about people wanting to do things the "old-fashioned way". Release date pressure is another obstacle to overcome. Companies often face the following type of situation: The firm really wants (or needs) to get a particular feature into the market. However, the automatic or continuous update of the feature hasn't been tested or doesn't work correctly. The developers say they need another month to get everything up to snuff. Then the manager says, "Okay, we'll fix the update mechanism next time. Push this update now and if they have to reboot, so be it!" But of course, "next time" never comes.

Lots of companies, large and small, are making decisions like this. At larger firms, it's not even a cost consideration anymore. It's about the time and effort to make the transition to continuous updates weighed against the possible delay of some products and features reaching the market. This is coupled with the reality that most companies aren't yet feeling a compelling need or the must-act market pressure to do things differently.

Becoming Continuous Update Curious

We're in a phase where continuous updates are being done more and more, and this is naturally bringing costs down. It's also creating improvements in how continuous update environments operate. We're seeing, and will continue to see, the development of more tools and more practices that make continuous updates less costly.

For all firms, making any significant transition is a cost/benefit decision. Costs are not always measured in dollars and cents. From a financial perspective, technical implementation of liquid software is already cost-effective. What's more problematic are the overall infrastructural transformations firms will have to undertake in order to become continuous update providers – particularly, changes to their internal, corporate cultures. Overcoming reluctance, status quo bias, and the challenging work of change may not be dollar-wise expensive, but it can be costly in terms of time, procedural realignments, training, and other factors. So, while purely monetary considerations are making liquid software the smart, competitive choice, we don't underestimate the very real personnel and productivity impacts involved in getting from here to there.

Firms that are not moving toward continuous updates must engage in a risk assessment that considers the costs of *not* implementing liquid software practices and delivery systems. Companies cannot ignore what their competitors are doing, or will soon be doing, on the continuous update front. At bare minimum, all companies must be continuous update curious.

Let Your Insecurities Melt Away

Then there's security. This isn't just a top-level concern for critical systems. Everyone is concerned about security. We have to contend with hacks, data theft, and other digital crimes, such as ransomware attacks. Liquid software must rely on signing and validation pass gates with full accountability, meaning it must be fully traceable. People must have complete confidence in these systems. Otherwise, progress toward continuous updates will be slow, and could potentially lead to larger catastrophes than we are already seeing in the old software environment.

Let's look at what happened to Great Britain's National Health Service (NHS). In May 2017, forty-two NHS health delivery services throughout England were affected by the global *WannaCry* ransomware attack. At the time, those facilities still had computers running *Windows XP*, an operating system for which Microsoft had three years earlier ceased to provide support and security updates. The NHS was not unique in this. Despite Microsoft's lack of support and the high-profile notoriety of the NHS hack, as of this writing, XP is listed as the fourth-ranked computer operating system in use around the world!

Why would an essential human service organization like the NHS take such a risk? Probably because their administrators felt caught between a rock and a hard place. They could refrain from upgrading and go on with the knowledge that at some point a hack could very well take place, or they could upgrade with the fear that some critical systems would malfunction or completely cease to operate. In either scenario, if the affected system were, for example, a kidney dialysis machine, they would potentially be dealing with a life or death situation. So, like so many other institutions and businesses, the NHS made the decision to stick with the devil they knew versus trying the one they didn't.

Businesses should not have to continue to grapple with these questions. Yes, security and accountability are issues that have not been comprehensively resolved – certainly not to the levels of confidence and trust we are addressing. However, without question, we must tackle these problems. And we emphasize that we currently have the means to do so.

Update Inhibitions

A common phenomenon among users is what can be referred to as the dot-zero (.0) effect. This is the update inhibition exhibited by consumers when a new software version is released. Based on their previous experience, chatter on social media, user forums, and what they hear around the office, consumers are justifiably cautious. They know that while the updated version may well contain many new and innovative features, those changes also carry a high degree of risk. We can address this risk-aversion by breaking up changes into smaller pieces, and making them continuous rather than rolling them into major versions. It's a best practice mantra of the liquid software revolution – release small, release often.

This impacts software vendors just as much as consumers. Vendors have come to expect risk-aversion behavior on the part of their customers. They treat their major version releases as those that people are *not* going to use. The experimenters, the brave, and even the careless put these versions into production, but vendors regard .0 releases as very transient and not very profit making. They know that if a big impact is to come from a major new release, it will be after patch versions start to appear.

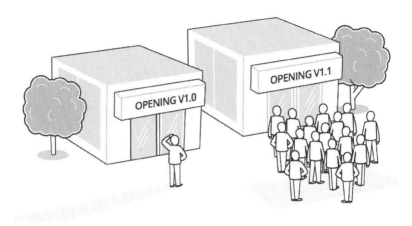

The "Dot-Zero" Effect

With semantic versioning, where there are major, minor, and patch subdivisions of a new version, it's almost always the patch versions that stimulate user uptake and an increase in the overall upgrade pattern. For large enterprises, the big boom frequently comes after the release of the next minor version. The assumption is that once version 5.0 has been released and is subsequently followed by 5.0.1, 5.0.2, and so on, the real stability will come with version 5.1 and above. So as we can see, the version concept extends far beyond the engineering domain. It affects consumer psychology and significantly impacts the business model.

It's an all-too-familiar scenario. Initial users are the guinea pigs – they're not so much software testers as they are users upon whom software is being tested. This saddles most of the burden of the update where it doesn't belong – on the user.

Web-based applications have turned this around. With cloud computing, users aren't at liberty to decide which version of the software they want to use. In these environments, vendors are in a better position to manage rollouts, sample sizes, feedback mechanisms and, perhaps as important as anything else, marketplace reputation.

Vendors can design dot-zero introduction plans intended for heavy testing. They can decide, for example, that only 1% of users will be able to access the latest version. After gauging user reaction and making appropriate adjustments, they might expand access to 5%. Monitoring, patching, and improving can continue until the vendor is comfortable migrating all users over.

The Liquid is in the Details

We've mentioned that continuous updates do not exist only in the future; they are in practice right now in many areas of the software industry. We've posited that more pressure from the market will encourage further transitions to continuous updates. Yet, liquid software – with all that it can deliver – and is delivering as you read these words – is still manual. The tools in use for making continuous update systems function are, ironically, manually operated things. So, there is developer work to be done in this arena.

This shouldn't raise any eyebrows. It's quite an undertaking to change an internal software development culture, adopt DevOps practices and systems, and implement the essentials to provide continuous updates. It will require further initiatives to mature the progress already achieved and get machines to handle more of the internal processes.

Pressures for greater shifts toward continuous updates and for continuous update systems to be more machine-reliant may come from two ends at once – from developers and consumers alike. Let's take, for example, Microsoft *Windows 10*. Based on Microsoft's public messaging when marketing this operating system, it seemed to have been architectured for continuous updates, even though it does not, at the time of this writing, receive continuous updates. Microsoft may already be feeling pressure from application developers whose software is running on top of Win10 to move to continuous updates. This would seem logical, since it's a lot easier for them to offer continuous updates for their products than it is for them (or, for that matter, Apple, or any manufacturer) to do the same for a large, complex operating system. If that pressure pushes Win10 to become fully, continuously updated, end-users will certainly take notice. This will place huge pressure on all Win10 application developers to join the liquid software revolution. And with this accelerating demand for continuous updates will come increased investments to improve the machine orientation of liquid software development.

Data is Hard

A major reason that database administrators (DBAs) shy away from continuous updates relates to fundamental technical matters such as database upgrades and object schema model changes. This problem is baked into engineering culture, particularly among database managers and administrators. Being unfamiliar with and/or untrained in DevOps practices, DBAs may have generalized fears of having to orient themselves to a new way of thinking and doing things, or of having to build entirely new processes. These professionals are under huge pressure from operations personnel to keep databases intact, secure, and capable of quickly responding to requests and answering queries. To ensure delivery on these high expectations, they put systems in place that are immune to continuous updates of data schema, data models, and data layers, and over which they may be supremely in control. DBAs are reluctant to (as they see it) lose this control, lest it result in disastrous consequences – in practice, and for them, personally.

All of this is at odds with increasing numbers of developers, IT professionals, and those in the DevOps movement who are singing the praises of continuous update systems. And it's not that these individuals are simply interested in the latest innovation for its own leading-edge sake. They understand that the pressures facing DBAs today will only intensify tomorrow. Paradoxically, as software evolves, the more they try to be the sovereign masters of data, the less they will be able to deliver on expectations for depth of responsiveness, versatility, and speed.

So, we're making an explicit appeal to those in operations: Learn more about, and seriously consider adopting, DevOps practices. We know you'll discover that there are sensible ways to transition to continuous updates and the use of continuous environment creation that will give you both confidence and comfort that data is being kept safe, secure, and always available for use, with no loss of speed to users.

Notwithstanding any preconceptions they might have, DBAs do not relinquish control over data through the adoption of DevOps practices. They can write a lot of the automation protocols themselves, which allows them to verify the impact of changes on performance, data size, the risk of data loss, and so forth. By operating parallel systems and maintaining duplications of data, they can run these automations on real production data before placing any changes into real-world production. They can also implement changes with the full knowledge that any required rollback is a simple procedure that will have zero effect on system performance and user experience. All of this frees them to concentrate on matters that are profoundly more critical. Instead of being gatekeepers who block advancements out of fear of theoretical damage that might be done, they can become performance optimization promoters.

There are still sectors that will push back on progress. Many companies will insist that they don't need continuous updates because their systems don't need to operate 24/7. For example, financial institutions and stock markets will say they can afford some downtime. They question why it's so important to adopt all these new practices. They wonder if it's worth the effort to implement a liquid software system that's capable of having multiple versions running simultaneously, while remaining connected. Why not just go offline, update, and then return to service?

Let's look at that question and reflect on the problems that must be confronted by firms that rely on cold system disaster recovery. In the worst-case scenario, all of a company's data storage and all of its low-level bytes are saved in another data center or with an off-site, third party vendor. All of the applications that are required to read and handle this data may be properly installed in the other location, but they are not running. If something were to go catastrophically wrong with a firm's primary (hot) data system – due to an update failure or a natural disaster – it would have to switch to the cold data system, which will inherently require some amount of downtime. This lost time may very well cost money. But here's the kicker: Most of the time, these cold system recoveries don't even work (certainly not as they're supposed to). This is because the cold data machines are rarely, if ever, running the same applications as the hot data systems; they never have the real code and actual binaries, nor do they match with the CPU, memory, and so forth, of the hot systems. The devil resides in all the details of small parameter configuration management.

In some instances, a recovery can take days, as entire departments of people work to get hardware systems (i.e., the network, servers, etc.) back online. These individuals have not been working with a company's main systems on a daily basis and now have to massage a misaligned, cold system backup into place. Even if every person working on a cold system has examined every parameter of a hot system and has a detailed understanding of how it functions, the fact that they've never run the actual hot system application on a cold system makes this type of disaster recovery a materially risky undertaking. So put bluntly, reliance on cold system backups and downtime updates puts companies at risk.

There can hardly be a more illustrative example of this than the $460 million bug that came to be known as the "Knightmare." In 2012, Knight Capital Group was the largest trader in U.S. equities. The company had its own automated high-speed algorithmic routing system, which was designed to send orders to the market for execution. Over a five-day period in late July of that year, the company updated this system's 8-router array in preparation for the New York Stock Exchange (NYSE) launch of a new Retail Liquidity Program. Seven of the servers received the new code. One did not. This human error was exacerbated by the fact that it had apparently not occurred to Knight that a second technician should supervise an update this important. We won't go into all the particulars of what happened on the first trading day for the NYSE's new program. Suffice to say that within 45 minutes, Knight had racked up a $460 million loss. As the firm began the day with only $365 million in cash and equivalents on hand, by day's end, it was bankrupt. By year's end, the company was sold in a merger that resulted in the creation of KCG Holdings.

This should never happen again. While a harsh, abject lesson was learned by financial institutions (and others) the world over, the point is that this is precisely the type of disaster that liquid software can help to avoid. If the Knight update had been liquid, its company engineers would have been able to see the update state of all eight of its system servers. In a continuous update context, they would have had the immediate ability to control version deployments. If Knight's engineers had been in a position to execute updates without downtime, they could have resolved the issue expeditiously well before the update went live to the market. This should be reason enough for companies that are still reliant on downtime updates and human oversight to take a good, long, investigative look at continuous updates.

Building Trust

We want to move beyond the era in which versioning plays a powerful marketplace role and causes real and estimable negative impacts on software firms, products, and bottom lines. To do this, we have to establish user trust in continuous updates (as opposed to trust in any particular version). The engineering of liquid software pipelines must include a comprehensive and systematic approach to software staging. It must also include granular attention to the dynamic interplay between development and operations, to reduce cycle times for the achievement of key performance indicators. This will require DevOps to:

- Adhere to its own creed of aligning its work with overall business objectives

- Coordinate tools and processes to achieve optimal tradeoffs for configuration management

- Identify the right balance between manual and automated processes

- Adjust delivery pipeline activities and process changes to the demands of businesses, not to discrete techniques

- Orient professionals to understand that liquid software delivery pipelines are not unidirectional, but omni-directional, sending data to and receiving it from a multiplicity of sources

- Foster the mindset that any single change will trigger a start-to-finish update process

- Use semantic containers for releases, which would include all artifact types that are versioned and executable, and

- Spend less time on "firefighting" (however edifying those efforts may be) and focus more attention on improving the reliability of changes flowing to customers

These things must be accomplished before enterprise customers will feel comfortable deploying liquid updates to their production environments. Currently, firms run a battery of tests on deployed updates to make sure nothing breaks. Yet production bugs and system outages continue to cost the business world hundreds of billions of dollars each year. For firms to trust that continuous updates are robust and won't crash their production systems, liquid software processes must demonstrate capability to deliver a level of quality significantly better than present update regimes.

Updates on the Go

Mobile devices and the apps that run on them have brought us closer to liquidity. In some cases, if mobile apps such as Facebook were not updated with the regularity we see today, they would stop being able to communicate with their servers altogether. To facilitate the need for speed, software companies have made progress in the transparent updating of all of their software clients to allow them to easily deprecate main server REST APIs. However, the flow of updates to smartphones and tablets would be faster if each app had the ability to produce new versions of itself, adjusting only what has changed inside the app, and independent of the operating system on which it is running. We can imagine a future where we would only need to rely on an update process that affects sub-libraries.

The Liquidity of Things

In the years and decades ahead, we will see countless IoT devices introduced to the marketplace. It is IoT – both conceptually and through consumer demand – that will drive the changes needed to make continuous updates commonplace. IoT's combinatorial explosion is an imperative that is making progress inevitable. The power of an IoT device lies in what it integrates with and what it seamlessly connects to, rather than in what it can do by itself. And what IoT devices can connect to is evolving much more rapidly than their hardware and operating systems can necessarily accommodate.

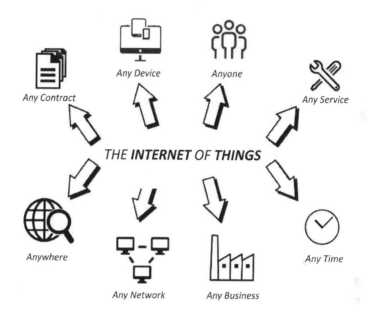

While some devices will be more popular than others, all will need to receive new versions of software that will allow them to communicate over Wi-Fi networks, apply security patches, make memory usage adjustments, and more. This needs to go even further. Smart devices must be able to "learn", by themselves, how to achieve high levels of seamless integration with other devices. Users already want this, but most are leery of the hoops and hurdles they have to go through to secure this convenience. To remove these obstacles, IoT devices will need more intuitive dashboards.

Our thinking must increasingly be geared toward continuous update deliverables in terms of "right customer," "right user," "right runtime," and "right process." Plainly, annual or even monthly firmware updates are not sufficient for devices that are interacting with swiftly changing environments. And regardless of when they're delivered, large firmware and software updates for IoT devices are equally untenable, because they are often communicating over low bandwidth networks with spotty reception, resulting in the frequent failure of sizable updates. Small, continuous updates, therefore, stand a far better chance of success. IoT devices need to be engineered as a set of small updateable pieces capable of receiving smaller, well-designed firmware packages via containers that are ideally suited for such miniaturization. Design standards must be focused on making devices capable of having small sets of libraries running separately within their operating systems. A lightweight package manager, such as *opkg* (Open PacKaGe management), can assist in accomplishing this objective.

You Can't Know Where You're Going 'Till You Know Where You've Bin

As DevOps has evolved, many advances have greatly facilitated software development. Branching was a serious and cumbersome issue for quite some time. Consider the development of the Linux Kernel, a project that relied on the Concurrent Versions System (CVS). The problem was that branching took an exceedingly long time to accomplish; it required copying all needed files into a special location. The software versioning control system, Subversion (SVN), facilitated branching, but a great amount of time and energy was devoted to pulling together all of the branches being created by developers, and to then executing SVN merges. This led Linus Torvalds to create Git, which essentially introduced the era of smart merging.

Software development has progressed from the age of manual deployments to the age of continuous deployments. However, if the liquid software revolution is to succeed, we must move beyond even this. Continuous deployment allows for the creation of new environments and for applications to be deployed to them. To achieve continuous updates, we have to be able to update a piece of software to the latest version while it is running on an active system, with users making active data queries and executing real-time tasks.

Some major players have made substantial progress on this front – Google, Netflix, and Yahoo – but many of their solutions are proprietary. What they are doing appears to be working well within their ecosystems and they are to be applauded for their vision and ingenuity. The liquid software revolution, by comparison, is continuous updates for the rest of us – for everyone. One should not need to have the whole Google infrastructure, the whole Google build, and the Google Cloud architecture to be able to continuously update files. There has to be a universal solution.

Drilling the Well of Liquidity

Software is considered soft because it's comprised of "soft" lines of code, which can be changed easily. And yet, software deployments and installations on runtime systems and runtime machines are more bulky than they are soft. They're made up of software packages. These packages are used by developers who share pluggable pieces of code and pluggable libraries. This sharing eliminates the need for them to rewrite everything from scratch each time they need to alter a particular piece of code. The JavaScript software ecosystem is a good example. It relies on NPM, an extremely successful package management system that streamlines the process of sharing and reusing code between and among developers, and facilitates the updating of code that is being shared. The idea is to package software into edible, well-defined chunks.

We have gone from creating very large software packages for which updates were rare events, to an age of open source software, libraries, and packages. These latter-day entities necessitated the ability to handle smaller sizes and generate more frequent version releases. This led to services being efficiently broken down into microservices, the development of which was supported by even smaller libraries. In turn, we created an environment in which new versions can be released on a daily basis.

Achieving these DevOps advances would have been impossible without the existence of tools that allow developers to completely destroy and then rapidly recreate deployable binaries with all of the previously created microservices in place. However, this only gets us so far. At present, recreating a big test environment that is populated with real data is becoming a tedious endeavor in continuous deployment environments. To achieve the full potential of liquid software, we need to further develop tools to better handle scale, security, and real-world production systems. The obstacles to be overcome before we can reach the goal of fully transparent and robust continuous updates occur later in the software build process. The great challenge for DevOps today lies in clearing those obstacles.

Don't Let Dependencies Drag You Down

It's important to understand that as libraries are getting smaller and smaller, they're increasingly focusing on solving highly specific problems. We must therefore devise better ways for them to be released quickly and integrated into the continuous update flow. The main issue with libraries, particularly technical ones (such as those related to logging or file system access), is that when a change is made within a single library, its impact can be very large. One change can trigger another, and significant bottlenecks are frequently created by the need to wait for all associated and dependent libraries to either manually declare the new version of the library, or automatically update the dependency graph. Then the libraries themselves need to be updated and distributed (sometimes manually) where appropriate. This process may be multiple layers deep, compounding the bottlenecking and delaying the release of software updates. While an entire stack is being updated, time and competitive advantage are being wasted.

DevOps cannot have complete confidence in the promise of liquid software without greater trust being built into these data flows. Developers must be able to rely on the automatic operations of continuous update systems. To some degree, the kind of trust we're talking about can be seen today in the development environment for mobile devices. The goal should be that whenever and wherever development is library dependent, dependencies are defined in terms of constraints, not fixed versions. When a particular dependency is defined by trusted constraints, machines can automatically execute version updates and confirm that nothing has been damaged in the process.

Testing for Continuous Updates

Software firms must have end-to-end, in-house, continuous update processes that optimize the work of DevOps personnel and the capabilities of software configuration management (SCM) tools. This will ensure that new, secure versions of software can be rapidly verified for smooth operations in production environments before being pushed out to real-world production use.

In an environment where huge amounts of data must be managed, and software is comprised of numerous microservices, customers don't have the means (nor should it ever be their role) to validate the correctness of updates.

However, such management has also become increasingly difficult, time consuming, and costly for vendors. For example, it's burdensome to set up a lab to carry out testing on a set of microservices comprising a number of Docker images running in a cluster that could amount to terabytes of data and gigabytes of database indexes. In years past, when update releases were fewer and the relative amount of data being handled was smaller, it was much more feasible for vendors to establish in-house labs in which tests could be run. Now, to execute continuous updates, labs must be completely liquid.

There is no doubt that we are already in a new age. Tools are being created and refined to enable vendors to efficiently establish and deploy automated labs capable of conducting quick and fairly complicated test scenarios. There's also no doubt that Docker, and Docker- provisioning infrastructure, are going to play a major role in providing tools for QA testing and the establishment of test fixtures that are fully liquid and flexible.

The liquid software revolution is about more than bolstering confidence in software quality. It's also about faith in the ability of liquid flows to deliver reliable updates. That's why high-quality validation steps need to be created and consistently used. To achieve this, we need to fully automate integration management (creation, modifications, deletion) and user acceptance test environments. And although, for simplicity's sake, we are terming all validation environments "test environments", these can be used for more than just software testing. They can also be used to obtain monitoring and real-world performance data related to all phases of the validation process. The Key Performance Indicators (KPIs) include: quantity of validations, mean time to obtain feedback, quality of validations, and the actual cost of executing validations. Achieving all of this at an optimal level of performance requires the capability to rapidly and accurately create the many environments needed to carry out validation tests.

There are several significant time considerations to bear in mind in the creation and management of environments. There's the time necessary to develop any given environment, the time it takes to marshal the resources to make an environment functional, the time required to place an environment into a testing array, and to maintain an environment's accuracy over time.

SCM tools, developed before the advent of DevOps, have been in use for many years now. Many companies use them, but only in production operation environments to create stable runtime machines for their applications. Developers have taken this to the logical next step, and have adapted SCM tools used for production such that they allow for the rapid configuration of testing environments. The immediate advantage of this is a reduction of the time required to develop SCM scripts used in the creation of testing and production environments. The intensified use of SCM tools is a best practice that should continue and be strengthened as part of how we handle liquid software pipeline flows. This strengthening must necessarily extend to **creating SCM scripts for fully automated testing environments to provide us with reusable scripts for continuous update production systems.**

To this end, SCM tools such as Chef and Puppet help to manage updates to a system from a current state to a desired final state and are useful in generating some of the data necessary for full automation. When it comes to validating new versions of software, it remains a rarity to see a Chef recipe or a Puppet module being reused to fully create near-perfect testing environments that can be rapidly run, again and again. And while other tools, such as Kubernetes, are accelerating the process of achieving rolling updates, and all of these tools are very useful in erecting the infrastructure for continuous updates, they still don't adequately establish the fully liquid architecture that we seek.

When SCM systems are capable of clearly defining what is needed for the execution of these tests, it will become easier to create new environments from scratch. Then, if a feature is tested within one of these new environments and it fails, executing a rollback to a previous state will no longer be a tedious chore.

Testing environment reproducibility is needed to effectively incorporate these capabilities into the continuous flow of liquid updates. Testing environments must be able to automatically alter themselves to allow data management and schema updates to be properly coordinated in the process. In other words, SCM tools need to be *software aware* – managing continuous data flows by "absorbing" and being "conscious" of new updates and their impacts.

These advances will help us establish an infrastructure that will do more than flow a continuous stream of updates to the world's servers and devices. It will give those runtimes the unceasing ability to take the software updates they need, and to execute appropriate rollbacks to prior versions when necessary. In a manner of speaking, we are talking about the development of smart software in service of smart software.

All Your Runtime Are Belong to Us

Users are frequently confused by the array of platforms and environments in which software can operate. We can relieve their anxiety by enabling runtimes to accept only the updates they can use, and to perform prudent rollbacks as circumstances dictate. In the traditional rollout scenario, vendors include minimum and recommended hardware and software specifications. Most people don't really know much, if anything, about platforms and environments. Nevertheless, the onus is once again on the user to know or to discover whether a particular piece of software can function optimally (if at all) on their devices. Liquid software relieves the user of this responsibility.

In terms of constraints, diligent vendors have always worked hard to test as many of the combinations of different platforms, setups, and environments as seem sensible for the vast majority of their potential users. But with traditional software releases, running all those tests was cumbersome, time consuming, and expensive. With cloud computing, it's a lot easier to run hundreds of test environments and parallel builds. This results in stronger parallel testing and, as we've established, greater flexibility and control over A/B deployments. Constraints that are built into liquid software pipelines flow valuable data back to vendors regarding their updates. This information can then be used to implement platform and/or environmental parameters into the updates, so the only users receiving a given update are those with the technical capacity to accommodate it. The user won't have to do the thinking. If it turns out that a software update will not work well (or at all) with a user's hardware/software configuration, the user can receive a notice on their screen informing them. This notice might also contain precise configuration upgrade recommendations.

Stop Gitting Yourself

Software development progressed from the manual deployment arena of CVS (in which branching and merging were plodding and arduous tasks) to SVN, which was an improvement, even though it focused on the wrong problem. Git tackled the core issues and set the stage for confident, secure, continuous deployments.

Git branching, Git merge, Git flow, and all the capabilities spawned by Git in general, pushed many late adopters toward continuous integration, and then on to DevOps methodologies. Git has allowed an order of magnitude increase over what could previously be accomplished with

SVN, and it's completely changed the way new software features can be created. In essence, Git automated the process of branching and merging. From a conceptual standpoint, Git was something beyond a pragmatic, operational solution. Being a machine-driven innovation, it heralded the liquid software revolution. It is software that facilitates, and significantly accelerates, the creation and improvement of software.

Git, and more broadly, the achievement of continuous integration, is evidence that we are headed in a liquid direction. We are creating more branches and executing more merges than ever before. We're even able to carry out continuous integrations of pull requests. These allow us the nearly miraculous ability to have outside code placed into a code base on the condition that it has passed full continuous integration testing. And this can all be accomplished before we would even think about branching and merging these changes into the baseline.

Even though continuous integration of pull requests is a proven and powerful capability – and it's something we know we can do right now – a lot of companies have yet to embrace this advancement. This will be a big component of our liquid software future. Many more firms will need to get up to speed with existing innovations, as they are the necessary building blocks to that future. And we've got to get going. Our need for speed demands continuous updates!

I, For One, Welcome Our New Robot Overlords

High-end web companies are very close to full continuous updating of their own websites. They're using Git for source code versioning, continuous integration servers for the CI of branches and the parallelization of CI, and automation for continuous and quite complicated integration and performance testing. However, the QA world needs to be reoriented. As things stand today, it's very hard for almost any software producing company to trust that a machine can reliably perform fully automated quality assurance of software with no human intervention.

Even at the very best companies, while many testing and QA processes (such as validating, log analysis, application path certification) have been automated, there are still tasks being carried out by human beings. Once testing has been successfully completed, we move on to continuous release, continuous validation, and continuous update processes, where we encounter more DevOps involvement. This is getting us closer to the heart of the liquid software revolution, and it's where tools, such as a binary repository manager, are now assisting the DevOps world in making tremendous strides toward establishing reliable, continuous, machine-handled pre-testing and pre-validation processes. Continuous updates in a truly liquid environment mean full, automated execution of the deployment steps every time a change of any kind needs to be carried out.

Software industry professionals are now intensely focused on the growth and development of configuration management and automatic deployment tools.

Moving from Manual to Automated QA

When we open a tap or plug an electrical appliance into an outlet, we're placing our trust in a utility provider. Based on past experience, we have reasonable confidence that external and internal oversight and inspection regimes are keeping utility systems safe from tampering and that we can count on the steady, reliable provision of clean water and power that keep our lives humming along.

In a somewhat equivalent vein, many different providers serve an enterprise software organization. Security mechanisms must validate the identity of each provider and confirm that the flow of software that is continuously updating our systems has not been tampered with. Trust is built into these systems through the incorporation of validation steps. Back to front Quality Assurance (QA) protocols and procedures must be established and rigorously adhered to. We cannot and should not be comfortable with continuous updates unless we can trust the liquid software that is flowing into our devices, systems, and data centers.

Currently, within DevOps flows, there's a huge barrier between continuous delivery and continuous deployment. It's the difficulty in getting people to fully trust that a machine can make decisions about the quality and acceptability-for-release-and-deployment of software for their devices. In the production environment, even when there *are* machines that have run complete and comprehensive tests and validated that everything is functioning properly, it is still terribly common to have a human being conduct random systems checking to revalidate that everything is okay. The software industry continues to devote a lot of time and manual labor to executing software validation steps. This is despite the fact that we already have sufficient evidence that automated systems are perfectly capable of performing these tasks to extremely high standards of reliability.

So, we now have software firms that do want to increase their output of new releases. They're fully aware that this is fundamental to future success. Yet they remain unwilling to abandon antiquated thinking and manual procedures that are preventing them from obtaining their own objectives. These companies may have full QA automation, complete with regression testing, and every procedure being executed by the book in picture-perfect fashion. They may have metrics that entirely validate that their automated systems are working perfectly. And still, even in the best of these operations, we can find human beings reading all of these test results and reviewing all of the logs. In DevOps, we call this the QA Wall.

Dear OS, You Only Had One Version

As opposed to development environments, OS packages will only have one version of a specific library. An enormous list of libraries and apps cannot be managed on an OS. The objective in this realm is to establish reliable dependencies for each and every library and app to assure system stability. We should have the ability to update OS packages (e.g., Debian, RPM, Mac OS X, Windows) with the constraints that have been tested. As a first pass in this process, all of these constraints need to be tested together. If all of those packages, along with their associated metadata, get past this phase, we can move on to the next step toward integration – the user acceptance test.

The manner in which libraries are packaged and distributed in RPM is an example of the type of confidence assurance functionality that would be a part of any continuous update testing regime. The objective is for the OS to connect to approved sources of OS packages that have already undergone all necessary and appropriate environmental testing. The OS receives continuous updates from these sources and the trusted data flows they make possible are an integral component of the liquid software revolution.

Images: Choking on Big Gulps

Machine images, such as virtual machines (VMs) and Amazon Machine Images (AMIs), aren't very liquid. Containers, such as Docker images (at least as they are mostly used today), are better, but still not fully liquid. Still, in their handling of enormous numbers of immutable environments and setups, software giants like Netflix, Yahoo!, and Google have proven themselves capable of continuously updating machine and container images by dedicating significant hardware and DevOps resources to this process. And these companies have been freely releasing to the open source community many of the tools and techniques that have helped them achieve success in the continuous updates arena. Examples include Kubernetes (originally designed by Google) and *Spinnaker* (an original creation of Netflix Open Source Software).

Nevertheless, the use of machine images will almost assuredly be greatly diminished in our liquid software future. To the degree that they remain in use, they will need to change to better accommodate continuous update flows. As for containers, while there is much to say about their design and about how they are being used by large firms, we think it will be helpful to understand, at least, how Docker layering negatively affects the liquidity of software updates.

The critical problem is caused when new layers are stacked on top of older layers during the construction of runtime packages. By retaining old versions along with newer ones, runtimes can become polluted with what is, essentially, junk. Over time, this can result in image bloat, which can impact update times. An alternative would be to rebuild runtime packages from scratch every time, but this also creates overhead in that reusable components are unnecessarily being recreated over and over again. The solution, in our estimation, is to maintain base images that archive most of these components. These would be used, as appropriate, to directly rebuild singular layers that include a given app's necessary components. This maximally efficient methodology would allow for fresh configurations for each and every rebuild, yet eliminate excess layering and update lag times.

Since image efficiency is often disregarded in favor of ease-of-use, when building container images, a longer-term solution may be to create a "flattened" image on top of a previous version image, such that differences are stored in an enhanced image format. A smart update mechanism could use these differences as a means of rapidly pulling changes up to the active file level. Liquidity would, thereby, be leading us to *layer dynamic linking*.

All Aboard!

We know what must change and what, inexorably, is already changing. Software firms are for the most part moving away from big firmware and/or software updates, and toward liquid continuous updates. From development to devices, we're on the threshold of a world awash with software where updates will flow continually. To holistically make this future a reality, we must have the ability to define dependencies by a set of established qualities, allowing us to automate testing and validate functions. We must also have constant streams of data that will inform how best to create, test, validate, deliver, and implement those updates. And reducing the size of our software components assures our ability to generate very specific and highly accurate data. So, let's get small. Small is beautiful!

This will represent an evolution beyond continuous deployment. Today, it's quite easy to release, deploy, and install something, and to carry out continuous delivery to a brand-new environment. It is not very complicated to issue a new release and insert it into a new container. What's difficult is executing real-time, rolling updates of databases and database schemas, as well as continuously and securely updating final running software with zero downtime. The liquid software story is really the extension of a saga that began with continuous integration, went through continuous delivery, and is moving to continuous updates.

CHAPTER 4:
WHERE WE'RE GOING

*"Speed will follow when the mechanism
of the movements is more assured."*
– Rafael Sabatini, novelist

Distilling Binaries

Since the turn of the century, we've seen an explosion of binaries. Unless it moves toward a liquid software architecture, DevOps will encounter increasing difficulties in keeping pace with the avalanche of code that must be now be written, tested, modified as appropriate, and placed into production. In a liquid environment, a promotion pyramid can assist us to obtain useful feedback to address issues as they arise at each step along the way.

The Age of Binaries
Explosion of Binaries

Today		IoT
		Docker
		Microservices
		DevOps
		C D
		C I
2001		Agile

With a promotion pyramid, we're seeking to stop the flow, so we can throw away bad versions of software as quickly as possible, while offering necessary and critical observations to software developers. This allows them to chase down problems, make adjustments, and return software to the production flow.

Looking at things sequentially, in the first layer we have unit testing. Our code is built, and a unit test can be done quickly because it's targeted to a small amount of code. This allows us to supply developers with really rapid feedback. Unit testing occurs quite frequently, and often on the local machines of developers. Every commit and every push —

everything that happens in source control management or any kind of VCS system, such as Git – has its own unit test, with feedback provided to developers.

In addition, some type of integration or development test is typically run. This involves a lot more code, and results in the assembly of more component parts of our software to verify that everything is being built and tested properly. Of course, this takes a great deal more time to accomplish, and it generates additional feedback for developers. At this stage, developers aren't burdened with running development and integration tests. With the rise of the machines, the system will handle these steps. All developers need to do is provide accurate and timely responses to the feedback – noting, for example, that since the last commit, an integration test evidenced something that was broken or done improperly. Further up the promotion pyramid, there are performance and other end stage tests, which consume even more time and generate yet more feedback.

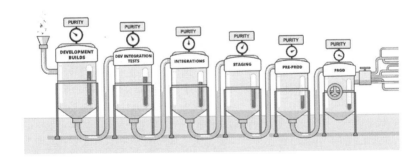

A Promotion Pyramid as Stages of Distilling Binaries

As we dedicate increasing amounts of time to each step along the way up the pyramid, we find ourselves executing processes that are actually providing us with ever stronger validations of the work that's being done. The outcome of this is a flow of binaries that gets thinner and thinner. The amount of binary creation at the first stage in the unit test is quite large, as every commit and every line of code that is changed creates new binaries. As we work our way through integration, performance testing, and production, the number of binaries surviving to be promoted to the next level goes down. By the time we reach the final stage, we have a really continuous stream of liquid software that has been created and validated for production.

It's worth re-emphasizing that the main goal at each phase is to rapidly generate accurate, detailed feedback to the developer. When any given test can be executed more quickly, everyone benefits, because feedback that is produced swiftly allows for the management of more binaries. As more machines precisely and expeditiously handle more tests – resulting in the generation of increasing amounts of granular feedback – we will be able to create more – and higher quality – software.

There are additional advantages to the rise of the machines. For example, if we have an integration test that takes two hours to complete, we can still carry out every other integration test by parallelizing these tests and having as many machines as are necessary to set up the parameters of integration tests for any changes that have been made to our code.

All of this must occur with zero downtime. Machines should not only run user acceptance, QA, and other tests on updates, but the tests themselves should be tested (i.e., mutation testing) so they can be modified, improved, and deployed to run against latest version updates.

Liquidity saves time, energy, and money, all the while reducing tedium. We don't have to start from scratch and do a full, new deployment into which data has been added as a result of feedback provided to the developer, and then run tests on that (and any subsequent) deployment. Rather, liquidity offers us ready-made environments upon which we can test as many and as varied updates as we would like, including canary testing environments. Machine-driven, parallel pre-production, user acceptance test environments make all of this possible. With liquidity, every system call that goes to any deployed production system can also be channeled to any system update that's being tested. This allows for real-time and real-world behavioral and stability checks.

Storming the Barricades

When we think of revolutions, we typically think of a group or force displacing an existing power. But the liquid software revolution is an upheaval from within. To create software, we actually need other software. The best people to create software that's used by developers to create software are the software developers themselves! These engineers create the tools they need – so they're well positioned to self-disrupt.

For a long time, software developers have been engaged in doing often annoyingly repetitive tasks. They sit in front of their computers, programming software to carry out repetitive tasks. They accept a context in which, by writing the code for repetitive tasks, they are working in an environment where the function of writing that code is, itself, a repetitive task. That has been the existing order.

Some people have come to rebel against that order, and so began the revolution. They said, "Enough is enough! Why do I have to keep doing this?" They decided it was time to write the code that would *carry out* the boring repetitive task of writing the code for repetitive tasks. We live in a computerized era, so why shouldn't that aspect of software development be computerized, too?

Linus Torvalds, *creator* of *Linux*, took up this revolutionary cause when he authored Git, which describes itself as "a free and open source distributed version control system designed to handle everything from small to very large projects with speed and efficiency." Git has significantly facilitated software development. Every developer's copy of the code of a given project is also a repository that contains the complete history of all changes made to that project. This is important for a number of reasons, but most significantly because it efficiently addresses the need to quickly push all of that information out to any and all persons involved with a particular project, rather than have each of them pulling it from a single, centralized source through the use of version control systems such as Subversion (SVN) and Concurrent Versions System (CVS). Git also allows developers to concurrently work on different branches of a piece of software, commit new changes, merge revisions and fixes, and compare past versions in an optimized environment that does not require network access. The liquid software revolution could not have begun without Git.

Other great revolutionaries include:

- **Ian Murdock**, co-creator of the **Linux distribution**, *Debian*. He established the resolution mechanism, apt-get, that made it possible to update a Linux Debian installation automatically.

- **Jason van Zyl**, founder of the *Apache Maven* project for modular software builds.

- **Hans Dockter**, creator of *Gradle*, the open source build automation system.

- **Kohsuke Kawaguchi**, creator of *Jenkins*, the Java-based open source automation build server.

- **Yoav Landman**, co-founder of JFrog, whose *Artifactory,* the first and only universal artifact repository manager on the market, can fully support software packages created by any language or technology.

Breaking Up is Easy to Do:
The Move to Microservices

For decades, software releases have been significant events, especially for widely used packages. Before the marketplace arrival of each there has often been a great deal of buzz and speculation in the industry press, developer and user blogs, and other places. Months of effort went into such releases, as there was a colossal amount of code that was being changed.

People spent a lot of time unpacking new software releases, validating their different parts, and conducting integration tests with current systems. On top of this, there was all the time, effort, and expense that went into user training, call centers, enterprise resource planning, and the like. Finally, carefully, and often with a bit of trepidation and crossed fingers, new releases were deployed into production operations. Each monolithic version of any given package was ceremoniously tagged with a version number, indicating the manufacturer's confidence that all major component parts were working together coherently. This critical identifier also helped support personnel to better assist customers with user issues.

Customers generally agreed to pay for these large software packages, even though many would only use a fraction of the functionalities packed within them. This was problematic for software firms because they were often super-focused on highly utilized functionalities. They rolled out new releases, which underwent extensive testing for these critical features, but less for other, more peripheral ones. Many new releases may have been ready for prime time, but perhaps not the Software Hall of Fame. Companies released new software versions with the full knowledge that customers were likely to encounter glitches, bugs, and even failures – mostly related to lesser-used functionalities. In essence, extensive real-world testing on those aspects of new version releases was taking place, well...in the real world. It was customer feedback that informed companies. Their solutions were reactive, not proactive.

Naturally, consumers haven't been entirely thrilled with this. In general, people would prefer to acquire or pay for software that accomplishes only the tasks they want and/or need to accomplish. If they find that an additional functionality is necessary, they're usually happy to add a new software component or an add-on. Whether it's software or anything else, consumers just want the products they purchase to work. They want seamless, transparent operations. It's not their job, and it's almost never of any interest to them, to know what goes on "under the hood" of the software they buy.

We can better serve these consumer inclinations by breaking up packages into smaller modules. Indeed, in very recent years, we are beginning to see software being sold in more discrete units, based on functionalities. On the backend of this, DevOps is focusing increasing attention on microservices, or serverless architectures, which provide functionality as a contract.

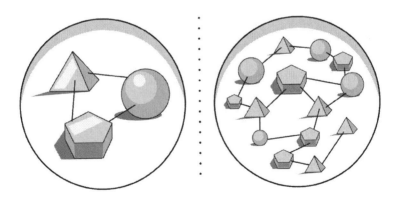

Breaking Up Software

We draw here upon the work of Sam Newman. In his 2015 book, *Building Microservices*, he sets forth the distinct **characteristics of a microservice**:

1. **Small, and focused on doing one thing well**

   Newman asserts that this idea is based on the *Single Responsibility Principle*, which states that any programming class or module should be responsible for a single aspect of a given piece of software's functionality, and that any service should be narrowly focused on that responsibility. He says, "...by keeping this service focused on an explicit boundary, we avoid the temptation for it to grow too large, with all the associated difficulties that this can introduce."

2. **Autonomous**

   A microservice is an isolated object, where "all communication between the services themselves are via network calls" and "these services need to be able to change independently of each other, and be deployed by themselves without requiring consumers to change."

3. **Technologically heterogeneous**

   Through the use of microservices, we can have "a system composed of multiple, collaborating services," which frees us "to use different technologies inside each one...pick[ing] the right tool for each job, rather than...select[ing] a more standardized, one-size-fits-all approach that often ends up being the lowest common denominator."

4. **Resilient**

   "If one component of a system fails, but that failure doesn't cascade, you can isolate the problem and the rest of the system can carry on working."

5. Scalable

"With a large, monolithic service, we have to scale everything together," but "with smaller services, we can just scale those...that need scaling, allowing us to run other parts of the system on smaller, less powerful hardware."

6. Easy to deploy

"Microservices allow us to better align our architecture to our organization, helping us minimize the number of people working on any one codebase to hit the sweet spot of team size and productivity."

7. Optimized for replaceability

As microservices are "small in size, the cost to replace them with a better implementation, or even delete them altogether, is much easier to manage" and thus "the barriers to rewriting or removing services entirely are very low."

8. Flexibly composable

Since microservices permit "functionality to be consumed in different ways for different purposes" they create opportunities for us to consider "the myriad ways that we might want to weave together capabilities for the Web, native application, mobile web, tablet app, or wearable device" and how consumers actually use software.

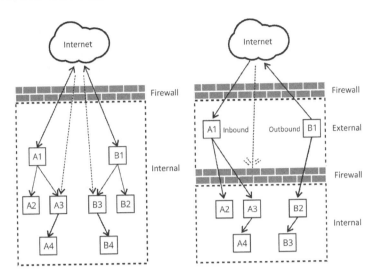

Securing Microservices: Internal vs. External

Microservices are compelling because they commodify security design and implementation, as their architecture makes the acquisition of discrete services a routine task. The illustration above shows how, in classic software architecture (left), coarse-grained function blocks are directly accessed via the internet. Propagation APIs are public, although sensitive APIs are reserved for internal use only. Microservice architecture (right) is purely public, with well-defined APIs being accessed by public-generated service calls. The microservice masks internal private services, which are bound by individual security constraints.

The continued adoption and proliferation of microservices is driving the need for reliable and secure continuous updates for services at every scale.

Great Things Come in Small Packages

The fundamental goal of the liquid software revolution is to create, deploy, and execute transparent, reliable, and trustworthy continuous updates. This requires near-flawless quality and security controls. We will have maximum confidence that our fundamental goal is achievable only when the component parts of the software we are engineering are as small and compartmentalized as possible.

A good illustration of large versus small components can be seen in Software Development Kits (SDKs) versus libraries, whose differences are worth understanding. These days, there are many libraries that are so big and complex that they function very much like SDKs. Nevertheless, substantively, an SDK offers a well-defined interface for developers, allowing them the essential means not only to direct software to operate in given ways, but to change the software. SDKs are more concentrated on interfaces and API definitions than they are on actual libraries and the administration of those libraries. An SDK needs software dependencies to be defined, since we need to create an API library in conjunction with the implementation.

The lines here are somewhat blurred, however, because there are no precise, standardized definitions of what constitutes an SDK, a library, or a set of software dependencies. We have a present situation where one player will declare that what they've created is a library, while another will say that theirs is an SDK. What we can say definitively is that SDKs, libraries, software dependencies, and packages of all kinds are managed similarly in a liquid software environment where the objective is the smooth and secure delivery of continuous updates. They are all simply components that are getting ever smaller and faster. It is most important to define the interrelationships between all of these artifacts, making sure they work together with good constraints, and operate in a stable environment. Then we'll be able to securely distribute them to the right customer, the right user, and the right runtime, each at the right time.

This Year's (New Business) Model

The pressures that are impelling continuous updates are also driving the need for a completely new business model for selling software. And the model for on-premise installation is learning a lot from cloud business models.

In many organizations there is a highly utilized high-visibility pipeline for software updates that exists hand-in-glove with the sales division. A major new version of software is released annually or twice per year, and this significant new update is supposed to bring in new revenues and create traction in the marketplace that will attract new customers. Advertising and promotions follow. Then there's a ripening phase. Most people won't jump on board with the .0 version of this new release but, after a while, when minor bug fixes have been pushed to the market, customers begin to upgrade. They buy the new version of the software. They pay service and support fees for it. This remains a common stratagem for software sales today.

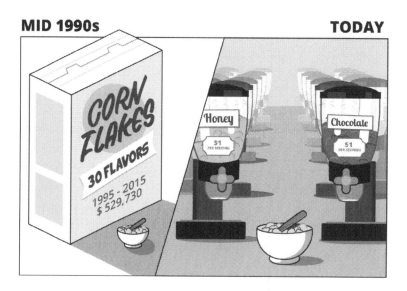

Changing Models of Software Consumption

When we implement continuous updates, on the other hand, we're selling software. Updating is no longer an event where versioning has a meaning in the marketplace.

In terms of sales management, if we want to introduce a new batch of functionalities, it's easier for public relations to fly the flag for a tangible version. The problem is that this takes us completely in the opposite direction of continuous updates. Most solutions to this dilemma exist outside of the traditional software industry, per se. They all leverage concepts related to the marketing of cloud computing, and allow software advertising to be unconcerned with promoting version numbers. Instead, it can focus on features, which can be promoted on blogs, in social media, through articles, and so forth. This is the future.

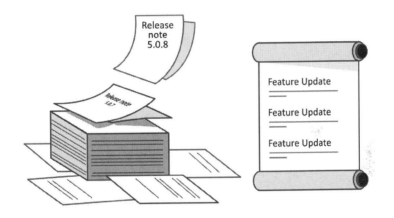

The same holds true for the management of release notes. If there's no identifiable version to which release notes can be correlated, what's the solution? At present, we see a compromise approach. Consider a smartphone app update. A version exists, but it usually bears some cryptic name or long, complicated, and unmemorable number. With a continuous stream of releases, no one is going to bother creating unique and meaningful names for public consumption. Nevertheless, release notes about these "no- name" versions (describing things like resolved issues, feature enhancements, and the like) are still being created, and are handy for reviewing what was running at a given point in time, or to see what new features were added, and when. These release notes, less extensive than previously, are small snapshots in time that track the progression and evolution of our apps.

Much of the way we produce release notes these days is automated. However, release notes are still being created for humans to read. In a fully liquid environment, we'll also want to automate release notes for machine readability. It's precisely the metadata they contain that will help us facilitate continuous updates. And we'll want release notes to be signed and certified, as this is critical to the reliability and security of all liquid software flows. Machines should not be reading or acting on any information that might be contained in release notes unless those machines can identify specific release note data as acceptable for action and as having been sent from a trustworthy source.

Rather than produce a set of static notes for a specific version, we could stream release notes, like a perpetual scroll, whenever a new feature comes online. As opposed to having a monolithic update of a piece of software, we would issue liquid release notes for liquid software. Then, every new feature and every new bug fix would come with its own notes.

We might think of this similarly to the way we produce streams of customer-facing Git commit comments, where commit logs are exposed to users, rather than needing to assemble them into more focused and discrete sets of notes.

Death to the Rebuild!

Here's liquid software in a nutshell:

- **Produce it from source code**

- **Do it once and once only**

Traditionally, when we have a batch of code, it is packaged up to move through a validation flow. However, in a liquid environment, we have the advantage of *binary-driven development*. This allows us to avoid having to go back to our source code as our package flows forward in a pipeline. The same package that's being used as a dependency is the one that's being run and validated. And validating a build means creating a testable piece of software (executable or deployable runtime) that transparently contains the previous package created. If the code doesn't change, then neither the package nor the testing will need to be redone. It's therefore the machine that's running the pipeline that needs to be programmed to avoid unnecessary repetitions of validation procedures.

We don't need to return to or in any way reread the source code as a means of recreating packages every time we want to proceed to the next stage, place a copy into the current production pipeline, or flow a package into another pipeline. These packages are just another element in our liquid software flow, going on to be tested, validated, and so on. Our solution is to create really well packaged software that contains all of the metadata regarding how and when it was created.

The result is an end to rebuilds!

To Err is Human, to Validate is Robot

Much of what we still do in software development no longer needs to be handled by human beings. Yet we still have people who are personally validating pieces of software. They review all the run data, using whatever tools they have available to analyze all the different cooking and stress tests to which software has been subjected – and then they make a *go* or *no-go* decision, just like a rocket launch. There's just one problem with that analogy. Today, most highly complex go/no-go decisions are made based on only a small portion of the enormous wealth of data being produced by machines. The amount of data that needs to be correlated and analyzed (particularly when that work needs to take place in shorter and shorter spans of time) can best – and in more and more instances *only* – be accomplished by machines. And the more we use machines to execute these tasks, the better they become at finding a plethora of issues.

It's easy to automatically integrate a new version of a service into a QA platform, and then to execute functional, smoke, and performance tests against it. The issue we're facing today is how to automatically decide whether version behavior, as a result of those tests, is valid or not. Our focus, therefore, is on machine learning. Much of this activity is a necessary byproduct of the fact that so much of human endeavor is reliant on software. Everything occurring in software development has long passed the point where it can be managed or, in many cases, even comprehended, by a single human mind. A lone individual cannot grasp all of the microservices that comprise a modern application. It's foolhardy to expect that one person, or even a qualified group, can or should be relied upon to perform all of the testing and QA processes, much less be able to analyze the behavior of an entire system. Machines must be given the task of identifying flaws that need to be repaired, and faulty code that needs to be replaced.

Along these lines, there are two types of machine learning to consider. One relates to test data, the other to flow data. The former determines if a version being tested is behaving correctly in terms of the nature of the test being performed. We need to know if it is functioning properly (functional test), performing as anticipated (performance test), stable (smoke test), and so forth. Flow data provides information to help us to best organize continuous flow pipeline steps. Tests in this area also include functional and performance tests, as well as static code and vulnerability analyses, cloud deployments, etc.

To facilitate machine learning from test data, we need improved automated analyses and feedback systems that are connected to QA execution platforms. Automated monitoring and artificial intelligence-based log aggregation systems should generate constant streams of data about the behavior of any given piece of software. In turn, machine-learning algorithms should be able to extract the core matrix of any particular flow analysis test and make go/no-go decisions. Integral to all of this are process backup and support activities, which can all be carried out much more swiftly and efficiently by machines. Just as there is a critical need for speed and efficiency when deploying and installing updates, we need to be able to execute rollbacks in an equally rapid and effective fashion when something goes wrong.

To facilitate machine learning from flow data, we need to improve continuous update flow systems that execute automated monitoring and analysis, and provide test data analytics. This constant stream of performance data coming from any given pipeline would include an analytic view of the control center (i.e., an analysis of that which is flowing, where it's flowing, whether anything has gotten stuck in the process and why it got stuck, where additional controls might be required, and so forth). This kind of granular, matrix data is fundamental to launching and maintaining machine learning protocols. Based on this analytical data, a machine-learning system can begin to initiate appropriate actions on its own, recognizing the need to autoscale here, downscale there, migrate data from one location to another, or even create a new location in which data can reside.

Don't Take Me Down

Microservices are strategically crucial for the efficient and speedy flow of continuous updates. For the liquid software revolution to succeed, microservices must be securely updatable with zero downtime. This is a significant characteristic of the Kubernetes platform today. Its strength is in its ability to correctly focus on the elements of architecture, load balancing, and orchestration needed to properly configure updates.

While having a REST API in place makes it easier to flow continuous updates to apps, our liquid software future will require us to devote more care and attention to database schema updates. Microservice infrastructures need to be able to offer better functionalities in terms of log collection and aggregation, sanity-checking, and autoscaling. To properly update the schema, they must be capable of compiling and appropriately sorting all updates that are connected to a given database.

If I Had a Hammer...

To be best prepared for our work, we're well counseled to execute a mapping of all the different needs that must be addressed in each situation. The exercise doesn't need to be exhaustive or perfect. It's meant to prepare us for situations we're likely to encounter in a variety of environments and at different stages.

We've all heard the saying: When all you have is a hammer, every problem looks like a nail. Whether it's continuous integration, continuous delivery, continuous testing, continuous updates, software configuration management, or regression — each of these poses different challenges. Each requires a different set of tools, although some of the tools can serve in multiple scenarios. When we're certain about precisely what we're up against, we'll always be in the best position to acquire (or, when necessary, create) the tools we need.

As we better understand scenarios, needs, and tools, we'll be better prepared for the world of liquid software. We'll have sharper insights into the inter-relationships and overlays of processes. And graphing these will give us the ability to comprehend forward and backward software flows.

Beyond the Trough of Disillusion

There's an old comedy routine in which a businessman who has failed disastrously in his attempt to open a new restaurant is interviewed:

Interviewer: Do you feel you've learned from your mistakes?

Businessman: Oh, certainly. And I'm sure I could repeat them *exactly!*

When considering what happened with OSGi, we take a balanced approach. We salute the forward-thinking pioneers who made it a reality. Without question, what they accomplished was ahead of its time and a welcome innovation. Sadly, it was really hard to use. As a result, it ruffled a lot of developer feathers and, eventually, in their irritation and frustration, they began to seek out and create more developer-friendly alternatives.

The stories of almost all great new ideas include failures. Smart companies positively *plan* for failure. Venturing into new territory means taking risks – calculated risks, to be sure, but risks all the same. Some bets pay off, others don't. The trick is to pay careful attention in the moment, as opposed to doing so retrospectively, when it's often too late to snatch victory from the jaws of defeat. In a way, we're encouraging those involved in, and those about to join the liquid software revolution to constantly update their own assumptions and approaches to continuous updates.

We need to reemphasize that this is not purely about practical and functional methodologies to achieve secure and reliable continuous updates. What you're reading isn't a cookbook or a parts manual. Rather, we're offering basic information about the types of things we must have in place to assure liquid software success, while also making the unequivocal statement that a significant chapter in the history of software development is drawing to a close. DevOps is here. It's a practice that's dramatically transforming the industry, and the time for it to be more universally embraced is now.

We are unapologetically confident in our assertion that DevOps is essential to liquid software. Without question, DevOps empowers us to identify development inadequacies, failures, and outright disasters sooner. This, in turn, allows us to execute adjustments swiftly and with greater efficiency, which translates into significant savings of time and other valuable resources.

Why are we so certain about this? Because DevOps is very much about open channels of communication and consultation. It fundamentally acknowledges that each of us and every sectoral link in the development chain has a unique role to play. Therefore, if we're going to be brilliant on the basics in software production and continuous updates, it's going to require all hands on deck, including engineers, IT professionals, deployment and configuration script writers, and other technicians.

DevOps recognizes that we live in a world that increasingly relies on specialists and specializations. We have areas of concentration and focus. And while this has its benefits, it can also cause us to become isolated from one another. In the software industry, we need to break down the barriers, working together in a more integrated and coordinated fashion. This should not be interpreted as a call for endless arrays of status meetings, which consume large amounts of time that would be more productively spent on other pursuits. DevOps shouldn't reinforce the way we've *been* doing things. Rather, it should be our pathway to perfecting the automation systems that will power the liquid software revolution.

DevOps is an affirmation that we *have* learned from our mistakes and are determined to evolve our professional culture sufficiently so those mistakes are unlikely to be repeated. And let's even take this a step further – this is *not* something reactionary. We're not advocating that everyone in the software industry sandbox should play nice with one another simply so some won't get upset. We're advocating DevOps because we believe the logic behind it is plain and unassailable.

After all, a 360° approach is just good sense. What would be the sound argument *against* rationally unifying all of the different aspects of software creation, testing, deployment, and management? Too many cooks in the kitchen? That may be a bad thing when trying to prepare a simple meal at home, but it's indispensable in a large, professional kitchen – where there's a need for an executive chef, a sous chef, a station chef, a pantry chef, a pastry chef, and a saucier, as well as a variety of specialist cooks. While it's true that any one of those individuals might be able to take on other roles, each is required to serve a specific function, such that the sum of their component efforts adds up to a greater whole.

The trend in the software industry is toward less specialization in terms of tooling, and toward more specialization in terms of component functionality. Full stack engineering, where professionals are knowledgeable about all layers of computer development, has become the norm. Although they typically have component level responsibilities, in principle, these professionals could work on anything. *All* of these software cooks are needed in our development kitchens. More importantly, we need to elevate and improve everyone's productivity through greater automation, integration, and monitoring, as well as through responsive, interactive communications. This will result in our cooking up better, more reliable software that gets to users faster and is less expensive to produce. In the end, everyone involved will be more satisfied with the processes and outcomes of software creation – including corporate leaders who are always seeking to reduce costs and maximize opportunities for profit.

We're standing our ground on the DevOps issue because we believe that liquid software will be the outcome of properly implemented DevOps. We're not being sanguine. We know that corporate cultures don't often change easily. Liquid software revolutionaries need to be advocates – not in a rebellious or subversive way, but as progressive champions of sound business practice. This can and should be done by using the same type of reasoning that is inherent to DevOps philosophy. It's necessary to better understand what other team members and partners do, and then to learn how to pitch ideas in *their* language and from the perspective that best addresses their areas of responsibility. Every firm has its resource gatekeepers. They're rightly charged with keeping a tight hold on the purse strings and allocating resources judiciously. Any DevOps discussion must address those essential concerns up front. Other arguments, regardless of how sensible they may seem, should be secondary.

Even with such sensitivities tended to, for some companies this won't be enough. Legacy mindsets and processes are very much a part of the landscape. To some, DevOps sounds like the flavor-of-the-month, something hipsters are doing. There will be those who believe that "serious people" should wait and watch. Fair enough. This type of thinking shouldn't be scoffed at. Rather, it should be embraced as just another language to learn. If the DevOps case is to win over the old guard, thoughtful and deliberate arguments must be offered about how DevOps is already proving itself, and why we're now well past the early adopter phase. Even that may not win the day, but we think this is the most respectful and intelligent way to move forward.

CHAPTER 5:
HOW WE'LL GET THERE

*"People think that computer science is the art of geniuses,
but the actual reality is the opposite – just many people
doing things that build on each other,
like a wall of mini stones."*
– Donald Knuth, computer scientist

Keep Your Hands to Yourself

The theory of constraints posits that when businesses focus intently on their weakest link(s) to success and then restructure to eliminate the barrier(s), their goals will be more attainable. Left unchecked, manual steps tend to proliferate, because human beings find these easier to manage. However, the more manual steps there are, the larger our packages of components tend to be. This makes our software less liquid and it becomes harder to unclog our liquid software production flow pipelines.

We believe that software producers should accept that the removal of manual steps is the fastest and most effective way to make the software validation process more liquid. The corollary to this is that the existence of a single manual step can generate a viral effect. There are numerous examples where automation systems were implemented for a large variety of tests, but somewhere along the line someone decided that a particular step would be difficult to automate, and a manual procedure was introduced. That's the first brick in the QA wall.

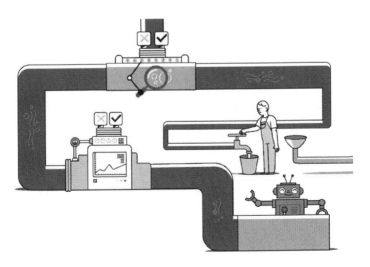

The Bottleneck of Human Intervention

This lone manual procedure frequently has a cumulative regressive impact. Others in the software validation chain, seeing that one manual step, feel free to tack on a second, which makes it easier to add a third and a fourth, and so on. Mandates that *demand* the avoidance of manual procedures must therefore be in place. Any manual step that is proposed must have substantial justification and undergo a rigorous review process before it is implemented. And even then, is must be deemed temporary. A plan to replace it with automation must exist, and the goal must always be to execute that plan as soon as possible. Automation should always be seen as the norm, and every effort must be made to seek automated solutions when individuals are tempted to opt for a manual procedure.

With full QA automation as our goal, human endeavor must be focused on writing and perfecting all of our testing. Humans must deploy and monitor tests to be certain they are being executed correctly. Our bots must automatically handle all of the system tests, which were once the domain and practice of human beings. Rigor must be applied to this effort. This means making sure there are always machines deployed, properly programmed, and ready to redo and revalidate tests; machines to read logs; machines to monitor system state and stability; as well as CPU, memory, and disk usage. All this needs to be tracked, analyzed, and validated by machines. Machines then aggregate all of this data and forward it to a machine capable of determining whether or not all tests have been properly performed and passed. When they have, then and only then can QA be considered complete, and updates ready to be forwarded along to DevOps.

The liquid software revolution isn't just storming the barricades of the QA wall; it's hefting a battering ram and utterly destroying it. The elimination of QA wall bottlenecks will assure the automated rendering of all the above-stated tasks. To inspire confidence, well-designed filters must identify errors, flaws, and bad tests, and be capable of providing extremely rapid feedback to developers about any kind of issue that arises as part of a fully automated QA process.

If It Hurts, Do It Again

There's a paradoxical way of thinking among many software developers: If it hurts, do it more often. For example, as we adopted continuous integration practices, the fixes required redoubling our approach to integration. The more we did this, the more motivated we became to automate these tasks, and the more we made machines do the work – our goal being that machines would eventually handle everything. The same holds true for continuous deployment and continuous testing. And it's shaping up to be the same for continuous updates. This is not a unique experience. Many industries experience pain as they move away from old ways of thinking, old ways of organizing, and old ways of doing things. Early days are periods of trial and error, experimentation, and innovation. Pain leads to progress, and progress is good, right?

Parallelism:
The Secret to Secure, Continuous Updates

The foundational aspects of liquid software are small, frequent, and rapid updates. The only way to validate and trust these updates is to have two (or often three) systems running in parallel (e.g., clients, servers, APIs, data sets), as opposed to doing things in series. We already see this in practice in a variety of devices and most everything that we do in software development, particularly in critical environments such as transportation and defense systems. These redundancies are absolutely necessary, as they provide real-time, real-world opportunities to test, adjust, and qualify updates. They also offer the must-have, instantaneous ability to provide seamless and efficient rollbacks.

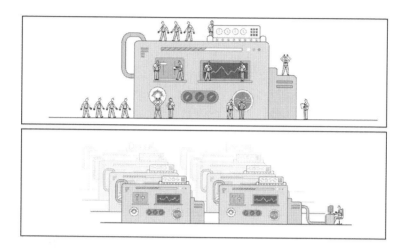

Reversing the Man-Machine Ratio

The Release Shuffle

In the four illustrations that follow, we look at our options for executing a continuous update on a single service, where each illustration depicts a theoretical Version 1.0. We'll explain how we can update each microservice component – service, persistence layer, client, and API server – in that order, to Version 1.1. It's a four-step process to update each, except for the client, which only requires two steps.

There are two essential rules to keep in mind at the outset:

- Systems cannot operate unless they have full connectivity between all components at all times. This is depicted in the "Initial" column (below) by the solid lines, which represent data flows that can be used to answer all client requests. It's critical to always have a connection from the client (on top) to the persistence layer (on bottom), regardless of any branching of the data flow.

- Continuous updates can only move forward one procedure at a time (as represented by the second to fifth columns).

Any infringement of these rules during the upgrade process will generate broken requests and make zero downtime updating impossible.

Each layer consists of multiple instances of a given microservice distributed over several machines, where versions 1.0 and 1.1 will typically not be running on the same machines. To accurately and safely manage upgrades and downgrades, it is best to deal with one layer of the architecture at a time. This greatly increases the reliability and repeatability of these procedures.

Updating a Service

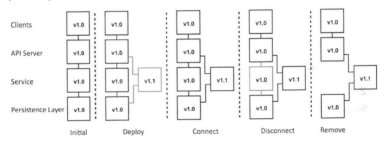

In the scenario above, we've chosen to update the service layer first. However, the order in which layers may be updated is completely flexible. As long as the essential rules are respected, we will be able to execute stable, reliable updates that can be rolled back.

In the "Deploy" column above, we see a service update process beginning with the deployment of a new version (1.1) to the platform that's hosting the application. The grey lines signify that this is only a deployment, and that the new version isn't yet connected. In the "Connect" column, the new service is linked to its two connection points – the API server and the persistence layer. This is the most controversial step in software development today. Developers are not accustomed to dealing with a state where two versions of a service are running in parallel. At this stage of the shuffle, API server requests may reach both versions 1.0 and 1.1 of the service, and the persistence layer can be managed by both versions. That's why the API server and persistence layer must be carefully managed such that they can make decisions as to whether to take their connections from the old version or the new one. Both versions need to be running, because we want to have the opportunity to conduct extensive, real-world tests on the new version. This will continue until such time that we can be certain that the new version has been validated for full implementation.

When the new version is validated, we can move to the "Disconnect" phase, where the old version is still present, but no longer linked in the process flow. The old version remains for a limited amount of time, allowing for an easy opportunity to execute a rapid and efficient rollback should anything go wrong with the new version.

If everything proceeds smoothly and without incident, we can move to the final, "Remove" phase. In this step, the old version is withdrawn from the system, the new version takes its place, and the update process is complete. Note that in this state the service layer is receiving requests only from version 1.0 of the API layer. This means that any new features of the new version of the service layer (in this example, version 1.1) will be unknown to and unused by the clients, as the client and API layers are still running version 1.0. Thus, in this state, the service layer has far more capabilities, although most will remain idle. To fully benefit from the update, all of the other layers will need to be updated as well.

Updating the Persistence Layer

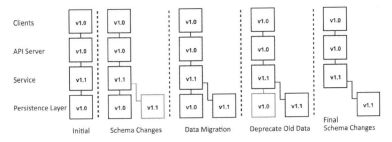

With the service layer running version 1.1, we can now update the persistence layer. And although the diagram above shows that the steps for executing a persistence layer update are conceptually similar to those used to update a service, updating a persistence layer is a very different process technically. The specific distinctions relate to whether the persistence layer is a relational database or is document-based.

The first step of a persistence layer update is to update the schema. For updating a relational database, this means adding or modifying a table or column, but still not populating (setting) or using (getting) it. The schema change occurs at the exact moment an alteration has been executed. For updating a persistence layer that is document-based, the schema change occurs whenever a new document or index is created. At this point, the persistence layer can accept data that conforms to the version 1.1 schema, but all of its current data is still in the version 1.0 schema.

When the persistence layer is capable of handling data that is formatted according to a new schema, the data migration step can begin. This step is controversial because the service layer must be able to communicate with two types of entries in the persistence layer – those that are in version 1.0 and those that are in version 1.1. For example, with a relational database, a new column added in 1.1 schema will have a null value for all 1.0 rows, but it will have data in 1.1 rows. In the case of a document-based persistence layer, every collection entry will always have its own schema (i.e., some documents will be in 1.0 format, while others will be in 1.1). This is why it is important to have the service layer fully updated to avoid the chaotic scenario of having 1.1 rows being managed by 1.0 service layers.

Once all of the data has been migrated to the 1.1 format, there won't be any possibility of 1.0 data appearing in the persistence layer. At this point, we can deprecate the old schema and any attempt to set or get 1.0 data will be treated as an error. This is equivalent to the "Disconnect" step in the service layer update (above).

The last step is to make schema changes final, which will force the persistence layer to manage only version 1.1 data. For example, in a relational database, a column that did not exist in v1.0 is now forced to contain data. This is equivalent to the "Remove" step in the service layer update.

Updating Clients

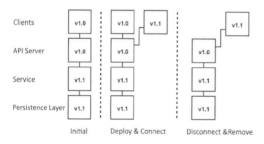

Here we see that client updates are more direct and immediate. Whenever a new version, such as 1.1, is deployed, it's immediately connected, due to the fact that whenever client code is running, its raison d'être is to connect to the API server. If a given API server supports multiple client versions, then over time an increasing number of clients will be updated to version 1.1 until eventually no clients are running version 1.0 anymore.

Updating an API Server

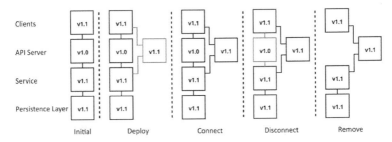

In the diagram above, the procedures for updating an API server are similar to those used to update a service. Once the API server has been updated to version 1.1, all new service layer features will be available for use by clients. Thus, the whole application can benefit from the now completed update.

What Won't Work, and Why

We've just described the order in which the components of a microservice can be updated. An analysis of the individual diagrams demonstrates why the order in which we updated those components is sensible. If we were to update the persistence layer to version 1.1 before updating the service to version 1.1, we would have a broken system, as version 1.0 of the service would not be able to understand version 1.1 of the persistence layer. Once version 1.1 of the service is connected, it will be capable of updating the persistence layer and managing the system state correctly.

When our service and persistence layer are updated, we can update the client. Otherwise, version 1.0 of the client will be unable to understand version 1.0 of the API server. With the service, persistence layer, and client updates in place, we can then execute the API update.

We should note that while the update order we've depicted is sensible for our example, there is, generally speaking, more flexibility in how a microservice can be updated. As long as the update process conforms to the rules specified above, we can be assured of having a system that is valid and functioning correctly, particularly during those crucial transitional steps when versions are running in parallel. This imposes some constraints on the ways we can move forward and on what we can do with code within given environments. However, within each of the boxes in the diagrams we've looked at, there is still quite a bit of latitude to make smaller changes to the discrete components.

The REST of Continuous Updates

The full achievement of continuous updates is going to be accomplished through microservices and the use of microservice dependencies and REST API contracts. This approach focuses on the fact that all the component pieces of a large app are comprised of microservices, which are connected via a well-defined REST API. As long as REST API changes are compatible from version to version, continuous updates of any given service will be transparent. Additionally, any new API will be visible to and available for use by all clients that interact with any given microservice. When a breaking change needs to be executed for a REST API, the whole system (any specific microservice and all of its callers) must be updated first. We will need to confirm that old clients are no longer using the old APIs. Then, we can break the contract and destroy all of the server's deprecated REST APIs.

This is a sensible way to approach continuous updates of microservices and REST API contracts. In other words, when introducing a completely new API version, new clients need to be able to select whether to use the updated version or the old one. This is done by client-first updates. In breaking the contract, a client is provided to all users, which can function in whatever language or system needs to use it, along with a new mechanism that can differentiate an old version from a new one. In essence, this creates a multi-version client that's capable of detecting which version needs to be in local operation, depending on which version is operational on the other end. We change the client first, and then deploy a breaking change to an existing microservice, or deploy a new version of a microservice. This methodology can be accomplished with zero downtime impact on the client and the REST API.

REST APIs cannot be written in stone. As with any other software, we need to have the ability to update them. We can then update any individual microservice and provide new API clients for use with new REST APIs, app features, or functionalities.

In a true liquid software environment, continuous update capabilities allow for forward-looking changes, transparent rollbacks, and the creation of shadow copies of any components or microservices. If all clients are capable of working with both the current version of a given set of services and an update version, it should be as easy to move forward as it is to make a decision to roll back. All clients should be entirely able to use a new REST API and then, if necessary, stop using it and return to the old one. Once we can determine that the new server-side API is not receiving any more calls, it can be disabled.

Supporting Multiple API Versions:
Client Side vs. Server Side

On the back-end of apps, we have databases and their schema. In a cluster environment, continuous updating cannot be considered completely liquid unless all versions are capable of working with new schemas. For example, we can add fields to a JSON object, a full table to a relational database, or completely new indexes. During a schema update, an old version of an app continues to operate with its old database, schema, etc. There follows a period of time during which we can have multiple services with different versions running against the same database. In other words, we can run an old version of a client against a new version of its database. Thereafter, a microservice connecting to a given database can be updated to the latest version of that database, allowing the microservice to begin using new features and new data.

Creating the seamless means to execute forward changes or necessary rollbacks constitutes an overhaul of the way people have been coding and developing software – but it's not that hard to do. And once people get used to working this way, it will become apparent how advantageous this capability is. It's wonderfully handy to be able to execute a rollback where old services are running against an updated database. Then, when the update process moves forward again, we can instantly begin using new features because there's no need to re-update the database. The most liquid way to roll out complex changes is to start with services, followed by schema, then clients and APIs – and then flip the switch.

In terms of API versioning, when we have an application that is comprised of many microservices, the only way to maintain a non-monolithic system is to have something that can be composed and decomposed easily. This can only be accomplished through API dependencies, which provide us with a high degree of freedom.

Services expose APIs that other dependent services use as channels of communication. With a proliferation of services we need to be concerned about the matching of a great many APIs and API versions, and exercise caution in the way we manage updates. The contracts between APIs must never be broken when we're running system updates.

The easiest way to avoid breaking changes to an API and thereby facilitate updates is to add new functionalities and features to APIs. This works as long as any new client using a new version of a given API is not communicating with any older versions of that API. We must be certain that we're only routing requests from new clients to the new API. This is done by pinging the microservice we're about to communicate with. The response received will contain the API version. The routing process can be automated as soon as the client determines that a particular service will be capable of using a given API version.

Maintaining strict API compatibility implies robust API versioning. This is not to be confused with application versioning, which, as we have emphasized, is on the demise.

API versioning allows running apps to know how they can use a given API. It's internal communication between software, not between software and end user.

Just as the liquid software revolution is opposed to software versioning – because hard-coding a version is always a manual procedure and therefore something to be avoided at all costs – it is also against wasting time and other resources in the creation of unnecessary APIs. We should think carefully before we act because, conceptually, new APIs imply changes to clients. Whenever changes are made to APIs, we encourage updating clients to be able to use those changes.

In many instances, though, APIs will evolve such that we'll have a version to which changes are incremented. We might even have duplicate APIs in the same version, where we will then declare the previous version deprecated without actually altering the name of our API or the version of that API. This may be inconvenient for clients, because it will only be revealed through a documentation consult that some versions of our API have been deprecated, along with references to the new version of that API.

A totally different and much cleaner approach is to use a unique URL for API calls. In this manner we can have APIs that are upgraded from one version to the next. This allows us to see services maturing over time and the evolution of APIs from v1 to v2 to v3, and so on. In this construct we usually see APIs that are completely different one from another. Generally, this occurs when we identify some fundamental error or design inefficiency in our original API. We would then want to introduce a new and consistent way to refer to given solutions through the construction of specific URLs, which access services in our system. Another option is to introduce a new version of authentication or a new system for the management of our API. (Although this method requires a

LIQUID SOFTWARE

140

major change to the way we would code our API and route to it.)

Data is Not So Hard

Often a software update contains (in addition to updates to the software and services) the underlying data structure of the persistence layer that the software is manipulating. This is usually a more challenging type of update, for two reasons. First, we can only have a single source of truth for our data, and we need to have the same data set available to work concurrently with all new APIs. We also need to make sure that we have no operational inconsistencies between our two sets of data, existing and new.

Second, our data set may be huge, so when we change our data model we may encounter issues. We can't always convert all of our data at once, nor can we take our system offline to execute a data conversion – it must always be done in runtime.

One very common data conversion method is to do data updates in parallel. This entails creating a new version of the data on the side, while our system is running. The system then writes to both the old and new data sets in parallel, for a defined period of time. This time is used to validate data changes and ensure that tests are not failing and that production can still function normally. Then we phase out the old data set and completely disconnect all reading and writing from it. We may opt to leave the old data in place until we are certain that our new APIs are functioning and our new data set is stable, and then delete the old data.

Another method is to execute data conversions on the fly. Data conversions of this type can be costly in terms of hardware resources, time, and potential risk. On the fly conversions are generally done online.

It can be expensive to alter databases (whether relational or non-relational), when that involves making schema changes and the introduction of new indexes. Such changes will typically have a big impact on performance. When we are executing database changes and adding indexes, we have no control over the speed and resources that are required to do this. This means that we cannot always pace down the way that an index is calculated. If we make a mistake in creating a particular index calculation, we may find ourselves in the unfortunate situation of having no way to roll back the change. This can overburden a storage engine and impact production in unpredictable and unstoppable ways. The usual way to take care of this is through the creation of read-only data, onto which we can add a new index. When finished calculating that new index, we would insert a switch point that makes our read-only instance the writable master, which can begin accepting requests from client services.

Data replication can bring a lot of benefits in terms of emergency data recovery. It's a way to execute data migration on the side. Even though expensive, it won't directly impact application performance.

Although less flexible and more difficult to manage, another way to accomplish this is on the infrastructural level. We do this by making sure that our routing rules are between new clients (i.e., between services that are acting as clients), such that they only route to API versions with which they are compatible. This can present problems when we want to remove an API.

When deprecating an API, it's typically very hard to remove it altogether when we have no control over our clients. However, if we're in an environment where we have full control over our clients (e.g., our own application that has been deployed as part of a very large cloud service), it can be feasible to deprecate APIs and gradually remove those clients that are making calls to old APIs. This is quite similar to the

API phase in/phase out approach where such client mapping is being carried out in parallel.

It's almost impossible to deprecate an external API. We could remove it, as we're not manually communicating with clients and telling them to phase to a new API because an old one is going to break. However, removing it should be considered a more fragile and risky procedure. The only sensible way to do this is to have good logging, which will allow us to inspect actual system usage.

We may discover that some API changes – which are, by nature, breaking changes – don't actually affect any users. For example, breaking changes will occur if we alter the name given to a parameter or execute some other change where there are existing clients. Even if there is an impact, an inspection of usage logs might reveal that there is only one use-case. We could then contact that particular user to make sure they execute a move to the new version of the API in question.

For simple object model changes, such as adding a column or a table, running services (old and new) will not be impacted or managed incorrectly by the presence or absence of data in a new column/table. This is where upgrades and rollbacks are easy. It should be noted, however, that it is very difficult to roll back an upgrade when we have changed the schema or an index. Those instances require careful planning and consideration about the impact of a downgrade or rollback. This is particularly so when we execute upgrades via certain types of data conversion. When a given system is very simple and there's no data conversion in place, it may be possible to flag an update as something that can be rolled back. In some instances, it might even be possible to do this automatically.

There are several types of data migrations that we might want to execute, and it's useful to look at them separately:

- **Adding a table without data migration**

  This is a relatively straightforward process by which we're adding a table (or a collection, as some databases are document-based), to a system. We can execute forward changes or rollbacks based on pure services, without the need for data migrations. In so doing, we're adding a full new class of data that needs to be managed by a brand-new service. This service will need to understand how to save new data into, and retrieve new data from, this class. If the data from this class is not coming from existing data, then it's a brand-new interface, such as a new entry point to this service. With this in place, new clients can begin to save and retrieve new data from a new table or document.

- **Adding a table with data migration**

  This process is a bit more complicated, but still reasonably easy to execute. In addition to adding a new table (or collection), we need to read, convert and populate it with existing data.

- **Adding a column**

  When we add one or more columns to an existing table or document, we're adding a new field with new information to an existing entry. Once again, this can be accomplished with or without data migration. However, in this scenario, the system needs to be able to read the entry whether data is present or not. This is because an older microservice will not populate the data and a newer microservice cannot assume that data is always present simply as a result of a column having just been added. When there is data migration, it means a column can be added and then populated from other tables or other sources of data (including external sources).

- **Adding an index to existing data**

  This process is executed to speed up data queries and facilitate the manner by which information can be obtained. Two cases should be considered here. The first is adding an index simply to speed up or otherwise improve the performance of an old system. This can be accomplished in parallel, on the side, without impacting the running system. The second is the addition of an index that is required because it would be impossible to perform some type of query or use a given service without it.

For each of the scenarios above, we should consider four fundamental questions:

- How are we going to update our database?

- How are we going to update the services that are connected to our database?

- How are we going to execute and manage any required data migrations?

- How are we going to make our system capable of accommodating rollbacks?

We also need to measure and monitor the actual impact on the upgrade process. If it's going to impact our data, it may be more sensible to have a copy of our data on the side while running our upgrade. As well, we should consider the impact any upgrade may have on services that are connected to a database. If multiple services are connected to a database, consideration needs to be given to when each of these can be fully upgraded and permitted access to a newly added table, column, or index. This way we avoid having to confront backward and forward compatibility at this level.

Our Valhalla: Zero Downtime Updates

As we've emphasized, the promise of the liquid software revolution is continuous updates executed with zero downtime. Basically, we're establishing the means to have an existing running system where calls to it are being properly handled while the runtime of the system is simultaneously being upgraded. As we discussed in "The Release Shuffle", after deploying and connecting a new version, we have a mixed mode scenario in which two versions are running in parallel. First, we create a system with high redundancy in place. Then, when we introduce a new version, we select one of the redundant nodes and begin serving new APIs to that node. This requires that the running system be capable of handling requests that are already in flight. When an upgrade to a new binary for a given library is complete, subsequent requests will seamlessly shift to being handled by the newly active update.

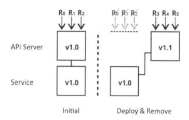

Updating an API Server with Downtime

Another option, particularly for online services that handle HTTP requests, is to deploy a new version alongside the old one, and then drain requests to the old server. Routing can be set up so both versions are handling requests until we decide that the old server is no longer needed. This is not an entirely liquid approach, as the full transition to the new server is typically achieved through the use of a timeout, which in practicality could result in some requests not being handled. For this reason, client retries are essential to creating the perception of server uptime. However, if the majority of requests don't last longer than a few dozen minutes, the transition should not negatively impact active requests in flight.

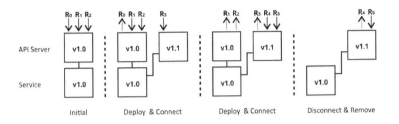

Updating an API Server without Downtime

Yet another approach is to inspect client versions. In this scenario, we have contracts whose task is to verify that clients match the several versions of services in play. This builds a degree of smart functionality in the routing layer so that newer clients that require updated versions of the software can be routed appropriately. Fundamentally, we're creating a contract through which the definition of a particular service includes designating the versions to which that service may apply, and letting the routing logic handle the job of making sure it goes to the correct version. Through this type of separation of concerns, if we can isolate each of our services, we can create routing that deals with each discrete isolation. This is a vital for achieving continuous updates.

Finally, a note about REST API, schema, and format changes. In a continuous update environment, it's useful to be aware of the distinction between two types of high demand clients – fault-tolerant and non-fault-tolerant. Fault-tolerant clients do not require high availability and zero downtime, while non-fault-tolerant clients do. For example, around the world, we see stock markets and banks experiencing brief periods of downtime every night to allow their IT systems to update. However, global web-based services, which are heavily trafficked around the clock, demand zero downtime. That's why web-based services use fault-tolerant clients, with the ability to display stale data when connecting to financial service back-ends.

Roll Back to Where You Once Belonged

Conceptually speaking, a rollback is no different than an update. It's simply an update to a previous version. If we don't think about it this way, we may end up with rollbacks that fail miserably. And when rolling back the persistence layer, we're basically executing a new data conversion to an older version of the database.

Currently, there are many applications that inherit their microservices architecture from the monolithic software packages from which they came. As a result, those microservices are not adequately encapsulated. They remain coupled to each other, and are interdependent. As a result, their APIs cannot support backward or forward compatibility, nor can they be updated using the processes described earlier in this chapter. This also means that these microservices cannot be updated without downtime.

When we have a bunch of microservices that are interdependent and need to run together, we may need to roll them back in one fell swoop. In terms of API and inter-service dependency, it could be tempting to think there won't be any breaking changes, and thus, nothing wrong with rolling them back piecemeal. However, if they all provide some type of service that can only exist when all the separate services are deployed together, then they create a higher-level component of microservices. For example, they may provide a better quality, highly available queue service by managing multiple components such as load balancers, which the queue service itself and some storage services are consuming. In a case such as this, it's very important to treat these individual microservices as a unit.

In terms of deployment and rollbacks, we may not want to approach the matter as something we execute for a discrete microservice or a unit of associated, interdependent microservices. Rather, we might want to view some new service deployments as atomic transactions where we implement an all-or-nothing phase in our system. This would then allow us to roll back all such changes together.

Containers: Taking Smaller Gulps

In terms of DevOps, in order for us to be able to deliver continuous updates, more work is needed to automate the operations side of the equation. Much of the industry is still based on continuous deployment. And it's not simply that continuous deployment systems need to be completely shut down from time-to-time. After all, in large complex systems, continuous deployment that results in, for example, a new installation of a service, is not very efficient. What we want is the more elegant and transparent continuous update approach that deploys a new version of a service on top of already existing data. With continuous deployment, there are significant issues regarding volume management, data management, data migration, and data processes. With continuous updates, we transfer these concerns to less cumbersome questions regarding load balancing. We enable our liquid software systems to read old and new data at the same time, working with old and new servers simultaneously.

Even the Docker solution for layer, volume, and update management – which does make continuous release and continuous deployment a lot faster and easier – is still moving us away from continuous updates. For example, as Docker currently functions, we have a serious problem if there's a security vulnerability in an OpenSSL library. This is because all of our layers could be situated on top of a base layer that contains a flawed OpenSSL library. Ultimately, with Docker images, we could wind up with hundreds of different images needing to be updated and recreated from scratch because of the need to use the new base layer with the updated OpenSSL library. While Docker takes us somewhere down the line towards continuous updates, it does not and cannot take us the full distance.

To bridge the gap, bots will need to manage versions and systems. They will need to be programmed to recognize that a given feature is running on a particular branch and has met all required quality criteria. Then the bot will be programmed to execute delivery of this feature all the way to the end-user. It's here that several processes will be based on versioning and versioning systems, though none of them will be human-readable. This includes the creation of a new base version on the master branch, new continuous delivery, new integration testing (including feedback generated as a result of these processes), and the final updating of all end-user software. In this context, and in terms of human involvement, all we really care about is the ability to deliver specific isolated features through the pipeline to end-users. After all, a given feature might only be contained in a few separate blocks of a piece of software that is comprised of several thousand blocks. To be fully liquid – to change a relative handful of small pieces out of a few thousand, and then create a new baseline for the system – all of these processes have to be fully automated and managed by computers, not people.

We've already indicated that in a microservices environment, mobile, IoT, and other devices can benefit from layer dynamic linking in the execution of updates. Operating systems, on the other hand, have historically only been able to manage one version of a given library at a time. The lack of standardized procedures or tools to facilitate secure, transparent, and reliable layer dynamic linking placed a significant constraint on how operating systems could be updated. To address this concern, the Linux community created a dynamic kernel-patching feature for that operating system, known as *kpatch*. As depicted below, it enables the

Linux kernel to be patched while it is running. This type of technique can help automate the last mile of Ops towards full continuous updates.

BEFORE *PATCHING*

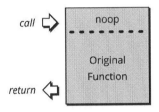

AFTER *PATCHING*

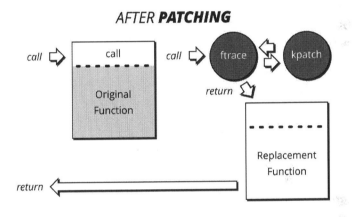

Live Patching an Operating System

This work is a derivative of "Linux kernel live patching kpatch" by V4711 (vector graphic created with Adobe Illustrator) under CC BY-SA 4.0. This derivative work is also licensed under CC BY-SA 4.0.

Testing 101

The liquid software revolution can never succeed in making continuous updates the norm unless it establishes a rock-solid track record of developing and deploying software that is reliable, trustworthy, and secure. This requires vigorous testing. Here's a brief overview of the tests that are fundamental to our work:

- **Unit tests** are fast, simple, and run during build time. They only focus on a single function class or module, and never span across multiple modules.

- **Security tests** are run more for static code analysis, such as static application security testing (SAST) and dynamic application security testing (DAST). This would entail, for example, source code analysis to see if we can discover any flaws, as well as attempts to execute hacks and introduce bugs to check for security vulnerabilities.

- **Sanity tests** are run to make sure that our system(s) will not crash. Here we're seeking to verify that all of the basic features of our software will function as expected. We'll want to run these tests for all of the many different environments in which our software is deployed.

- **Smoke tests** have more to do with resources and hardware, and are very much concerned with performance and sizing.

- **Integration tests** are run to verify that all of our functions will work together harmoniously when all the component pieces of our software are deployed.

- **Load tests** place a set of services under a heavy load to monitor anticipated performance and behavior under stress.

- **Canary tests** allow us to deploy a software update or a new software version directly into production. There are two ways to do this. The first is to make it a type of silent or mute deployment that allows the update/new version to handle active user requests. These can then be executed in a manner that's harmless to the system (i.e., nothing about the system state changes) because we disable our application from being able to write anything to the system. What we're doing is multiplexing our client requests. Any incoming call goes to our regular API and into the canary version. We then read the output from the canary version, to look for errors, inconsistencies, or incompatibilities. The other, more common type of canary test involves direct deployment of a new version, after which a subset of users is allowed to run against the new API. We can think of these as "friendly users" or even beta testers who will have a certain tolerance level for errors, should anything go wrong. It should be emphasized that this type of canary test can be quite hard to execute and requires discipline in its manner of execution.

Today, some extremely large companies never test in a pre-production environment. Google, for example, always tests in production, because they have sufficient users and environments to allow use of a very small percentage sample size of active user requests to conduct live, real-time testing. They place a new version or a new system in production, and if something goes wrong they just kill the servers that are hosting those new items. Users then seamlessly shift back to executing requests on the old version/system. Google never fully places something new into production until they are as certain as can be that new items will function properly.

All of these tests are independent of one another and don't need to be introduced into our *direct* liquid software flows. Rather, they can (and most often should) be run in parallel. The results of these tests will provide us with metadata and signature data. This information will be added as part of our continuous update flow when we are satisfied that a particular update is ready for delivery and the end-user is prepared to deploy it.

Unless we're dealing with a web-based service that we control, when we're in delivery mode we're crossing into the user's frontier. Accordingly, the liquid software we deliver must have metadata sufficient to enable an edge device to automatically deploy and use our continuous updates. There are a variety of environments into which an end-user may deploy an update. It may be an acceptance test, pre-production, or production. Of course, once an update has been deployed by the end-user, we no longer have the ability to execute a stop or a rollback.

We typically run stress and load tests to achieve quality of performance for a given piece of software or any particular update. These are repetitive trials that match the real usage of end users as closely as possible. We run these tests on a range of platforms, on a variety of hardware, and in diverse environments. From these efforts, we extract an extremely large set of data points. In a continuous update environment, a software vendor will use those data points (where and as appropriate) as metadata to be packaged and sent as part of an update. The software consumer will receive this metadata through a pipeline that has been programmed to recognize that specific software provider, if and only if the software being sent bears specific signatures. Thereafter, the metadata will be used by the consumer's device(s) to determine whether an update should continue its liquid flow to actual execution. If the metadata doesn't match the consumer's pipeline programming for performance and sizing requirements, then the update will be rejected.

What's Wrong with You?

We need to be very precise with regard to security data and security vulnerabilities. Ideally, after having undergone screening for specific security data, our newly created piece of software or update would have been validated as having no problems. However, in a case where our systems had detected and flagged the presence of a security issue, our liquid software infrastructure would refuse to allow the new software or update to continue to flow. Instead, it would be forked to a specified location where more security testing would be performed or additional development work would be carried out.

This type of pipe-blocking is great when we know what we're looking for. However, there are many times when software with no known security issues goes into production, gets deployed, and reaches the consumer, and thereafter some security test is run and an issue is suddenly discovered. In a liquid software environment, for our automatic pipeline validation systems to operate at peak efficiency, we must be able to immediately flag such vulnerabilities, and communicate swiftly with all the different places where insecure software may have been deployed and running.

This is all about backflow. When our liquid systems deliver a specific piece of software or an update all the way to production, we need our pipes to send deployment information back to software producers so they can keep track of where a specific piece of software of a specific service version has been deployed and is running.

Ain't Nuthin' Like the Real Thing

Continuous updates are the wave of the future. We haven't the least doubt that it's the most rapid, reliable, and secure method of software delivery. But that's still not enough! We also want continuous updates to produce software that's highly responsive to user needs and desires. For that, we need to develop and test software that is as close to the user context as possible. The only way to get there is through automation. It's essential that we capture as much data and contextual information as we can from the user environment, and only machines are able to collect, process, and filter such high volumes of data and provide efficient analytics. With those analytics at our fingertips we can maximize the efficiency and frequency of software updates in production.

A lot of web-based services run by major firms such as Google, Netflix, Yahoo, and Apple, are already doing this. They have a high level of confidence in their ability to recreate context, because the context exists in-house, captured by their own information systems, and instantly available. Unfortunately, there are many software customers whose data is not being captured in sufficient quantity or in a predictable, repetitive manner. The liquid software revolution must include vigorous advocacy for the construction and maintenance of information systems with the capacity to collect and process vast amounts of anonymized user data. The more real-world data that is available to developers, the easier it will be to create software solutions that are tailor-made to context.

Fighting Corruption

Determining whether an update will destroy our data is one of the critical validation steps in a continuous update environment. To be certain, software must be run through a vigorous series of update and continuous update tests, using a peak data set and a large-scale environment. This is important because we want to know the amount of time it takes to execute a validated update from one version to another, and that no issues are being reported for our given type and size of dataset.

It's always desirable to obtain a variety of different metrics about upgrades and update processes, about microservices that have been degraded, about various types of data, and so on. Examples include before and after upgrade/update comparisons of database data set sizes (total, per table, per collection, etc.) and JSON payloads (size, number of rows, number of fields, etc.) on high throughput queries (findAll and similar). And we want to be able to compare the information we obtain from one version to another. All of this can help to fortify continuous update systems, as this analytical information allows us to make optimal decisions regarding how liquid software should flow and be deployed, such that data will not be lost during an upgrade process.

To Infinity and Beyond

Automation should also enable us to establish and deploy as many validation procedures as we wish, and to handle as much data and metadata as we desire. Having no limitations on the filters through which our liquid software must pass will significantly increase our opportunities to improve the quality of the products flowing through our continuous update pipelines. Our systems must properly tag these products with the results generated from sanity, smoke, and other tests. To illustrate, these results might indicate that the basic functioning of a given system was tested, and that over a two-hour period, 50 users continuously accessed the system, which behaved correctly in terms of hardware resources and response time. This information can help us to better understand system performance and to carry out performance analyses that provide recipients of liquid software with sizing information, estimations, and risk management assessments.

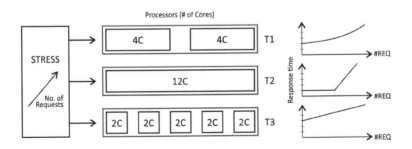

How Hardware Configuration Impacts Application
Stress Test Response Times

To establish appropriate management parameters, it's extremely valuable to run data performance tests for certain amounts of data, for number of new records created per second, for execution of indexing, etc. The results of these tests can help us establish a baseline for liquid software recipient sizing and, fundamentally, whether hardware and hardware resources are capable of handling any given update that might be pushed to them. If sizing data reveals a mismatch, the recipient can either increase capacity on their end or decide that a given type of software is not suitable because it won't achieve desirable performance results. Running continuous performance tests on every version and on numerous hardware configurations enables us to compare response times in a variety of environments from version to version. This can instill a high level of trust in our continuous update recipients.

Suspicious Minds

There is a growing field whose attention is laser-targeted on validating software for penetration tests and security data. These can be based on static code, running code, basic hacking mechanisms, and even advanced, automated hacking mechanisms seeking access to REST APIs and systems. All of these tests can provide tremendously important metadata to developers that can help them make internal decisions as to whether a piece of software can be released or not, and to provide clear, concise instructions regarding security setup (e.g., whether a particular API should be protected at the firewall or load balancing level).

Try Before You Fly

Pre-flight testing is conducted when we have a new version of a component that is a dependency of many others. This testing an integral part of a continuous update system. Our goal is to execute a change, but we have no idea how much that change will impact other parts of the system or other applications. So, in this situation, we would establish a pre-flight testing option that forks our flow to the sub-dependency environment, allowing us to check the impact of the new version on all other builds and all other tests that are being run.

All of the pre-flight tests we run, and all of the results they generate would, of course, not affect the people actively developing, deploying, and using this particular application. This would only be a change to one of our own local infrastructure components. We would work in this branched environment and run all necessary tests until everything passes muster. Pre-flight testing is an especially good way of enabling even extensive changes to be made via continuous updates of underlying components with the full confidence that all activity will be isolated, well-measured, and have no impact on the rest of the system. It also provides very accurate feedback about the impact(s) of a change and which other systems will need to be altered or adapted if there is no way of avoiding such impact(s).

In parallel, we would constantly run monitoring or "watchdog" tests within all environments. These tests would scan for fundamental metrics – restarts, memory consumption, request processing, throughput, and network latency – that go beyond functionality or business logic as a means of ensuring smooth rollout updates. If an update produces a significant change to any one of these metrics, a red flag would be triggered and the update invalidated.

Bringing the Canary Back to Life

After software has been tested in a DevOps sandbox environment, it can often be sensible to perform a canary test, which allows us to obtain very rapid analytical feedback. Without necessarily responding to a direct customer request, programming code changes can be pushed out universally or to a limited group of end-users. We can then conduct a quick behavioral analysis of the changes, and any impacts we observe (positive or negative) will be small and containable. This reduces risk, as it preserves our ability to swiftly reroute users back to the old version (shadow copy) if a test evidences any bugs. This ability is the holy grail of automated quality management and the only way to ensure smooth operations without the need to have professionals on-call 24/7 in case of disaster.

Since anything being updated may need to be rolled back rapidly and efficiently, the different versions and solutions must be close to the devices and machines that are operating the software. A binary repository manager offers DevOps an edge in this area. It provides an effective means for firms to keep, maintain, and deliver multiple valid versions of client and server libraries of a given API, with the different versions of web answers and different versions of clients all in a single repository. This dramatically enhances a company's ability to perform continuous updates of all parts of a piece of software.

Rolling Back a Release without Downtime

The most important thing is that software should always be updatable. Anything that would hinder or entirely impede this ability *must* be mitigated. We'd go so far as to insist: "If it's not updatable, it's *not* software!" When updating isn't possible, devices die.

Going Meta

One of the principal reasons that liquid software can generate economies of scale is the fact that continuous updates can be used within the processes of validation as a means of validating the validation process itself! (Whoa, dude! Meta.) The longer a liquid software architecture is in operation, the greater the time and cost economies it will produce. After creating a user acceptance test environment, for example, we will expect to compile a large amount of data from a lot of real users. This will allow us to generate reproducible environments, which themselves can be continuously updated with versions of a given application. We could then execute a type of copy and branch, and update that system to see how it responds. Then we could roll back the system data to the way it was before that update was applied, wait for the next update to arrive, and run a new test. In other words, we would be continuously testing our continuous update system.

Going meta can have huge, positive results on optimization and bottom line business performance.

Signing Liquid Software Pipes

Validation procedures are critical to liquid software flows. The output of validation procedures must be signed. We need to know and trust that a specific step was executed and that the liquid flowing through a continuous update pipeline is "clean."

In a fully liquid, continuous update environment, we need to consider the possibility of establishing some type of security API standardization, which can be pushed out to end-users to enable an automated signing authority the ability to certify software. More attention needs to be paid to things such as warranty terms, release notes, and client-side recognition. A series of approved signatures would be secured as part of machine-driven processes regarding QA, security, performance, integration testing, and release notes. Customers that feel confident about these systems and the quality of the user experiences that are being delivered to them can then agree to be connected to liquid software pipelines. They would have the full knowledge and assurance that the continuous updates they receive are being certified by competent and well-vetted processes, with all necessary and appropriate signatures automatically being obtained along the way. Customers could also be offered options to filter these pipes, and to make choices regarding which updates they get. The goal is to create trust in the liquid communications that take place between companies, and in so doing, to relieve end-users of human-intervention burdens.

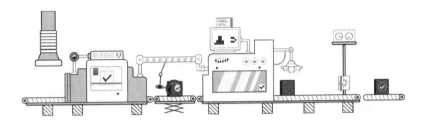

All of this requires high degrees of trust. Specific versions of software packages should be automatically tagged as certified after passing QA, integration and security testing, etc.

We truly believe that a global, open source API for software metadata (such as Grafeas) will enable this trust.

Show Me Where You've Bin

Many organizations have already constructed fairly sophisticated pipelines to ensure that the production of their software can proceed in an automated way. Such pipelines should involve staging. Think, for example, of an application that can run on an iOS or Android operated cellular device. The first stage in the pipeline would consist of a unit test, followed by a more elaborate integration test. Thereafter, there could be a stage that includes several integration tests that require specific hardware to test the software (e.g., robots installing and testing the software on an iPad). This would be followed by a stage in which artifacts are pushed to an app center – either an internal one for organizational use only, or a public access app store.

We want to verify the provenance of the software components we use in these different phases because we don't want any rogue user, or even a mistake in configuration, to push something along that will end up in a pipeline stage where it shouldn't be. Trust is once again the name of the game with liquid software. We need to be certain that the provenance of artifacts is only from certified sources, through digital signatures that establish a trusted chain of custody for the artifacts.

Security concerns are an issue for software that ends up in production. As software pipelines are being constructed, we're beginning to see customer confidence grow. Builders are making sure that every stop along the way within a given pipeline has its own private and public keys, where the private key is used to sign artifacts before they are promoted to the next phase of testing. The next phase can be in the same data center or in a data center located in another part of the world. The important thing is that the other data center (aka target data center or target stop) in the pipeline can always verify that artifacts being pushed to it were signed by the private key of the certified source(s) because it has the public key of those sources installed. The certificate (signature) chain that runs between signing stops is somewhat analogous to a blockchain, such as a Bitcoin ledger.

Plainly, having a certificate chain – a chain of trust that travels with artifacts – is far preferable and far more secure than the way these procedures have been implemented previously. Until quite recently, we would control the gateway to our platform by deploying a specific username and password. Alternatively, we would have a set of firewall rules that permitted an IP address, or a range of IP addresses, to deploy to our infrastructure. A certificate chain, on the other hand, provides us with a proof of provenance for an artifact regardless of the infrastructure that's in place.

The concept of signed software is not a new one, of course, and people have been executing signatures in many different ways for a number of years. In a liquid software environment, however, signatures need to be produced by machines at every stage, including for contractual matters. We must be able to sign liquid software with specific signatures for specific steps and specific metadata, which are specifically labeled.

Once we have all those signatures on our liquid software, the next goal is the creation of signed pipes that can filter the liquid based on those signatures. Such a filter would establish automatic permission parameters (e.g., "send through this pipeline everything that is going through another pipeline, but only if the software was signed by 'x' company and is accompanied by 'y' security label, and contains performance data that satisfies a particular set of performance requirements). This type of signed pipeline would create a type of unbreakable contract that could establish trust across companies. It also means that when something doesn't go through the pipeline, or something does go through the pipeline but arrives with some issue, there's transparency built into the system, allowing for fast and efficient tracking.

Robust tracking means that all metadata related to filters, as well as all metadata related to that which is present in (or has been removed from) any given pipeline, must be readable and queryable, with versioning information ("at this time last week software passed through this pipeline, which contained this specific metadata"). Looking at the history of the metadata that flowed through a specific pipeline is a much more transparent and targeted way to see what is occurring within a specific system. It's far more accurate than, for example, looking at the release notes for version 4 of software X, and trying to manually filter out necessary usage information.

With signatures, we also need to concern ourselves with contractual and business model behavior – using signatures when one company signs a software provision contract with another. The result would be a pipeline through which only the software that satisfies the terms of the provisioning agreement would flow. In other words, the pipeline would contain all the filters that are part of this contract, which would represent an End-User License Agreement (EULA) by the receiving party against the legal agreement it signed with the provisioning party. All of the liquid software that would pass through this contractual pipeline and into the environment of the receiving party would be signed, establishing a fully defined relationship between the software producer and the software consumer.

The More I Know You, The More I Like You

In a versionless software future, we will need a way to coordinate what is currently running with new software that is updating it. Automated mechanisms that install the new updates flowing through liquid software pipelines must be able to determine which updates are compatible and/or desirable.

Next, there must be transparency and coordination of all metadata flowing through our pipelines. We want as much reliable, actionable metadata and information about our liquid software as machines are capable of producing. The more information available to consumers, the greater will be their capability to verify the quality of liquid software flows and to design preferences tailored to their precise needs. The goal is always to be able to read and trust the metadata associated with the liquid, particularly as a means of enumerating and validating options.

With so much metadata reliably at our disposal, we could design a bleeding edge test environment in which we'd get the latest updates, *even if* they have not been fully tested, or contain no third-party handles. We might want to do this so we could test a brand new feature and see how it behaves, with the full knowledge that we're operating in an unstable, bleeding edge test environment. This way, we would establish a connection to our liquid software provisioning pipeline with filter definitions that clearly state our desire to get the latest and best version, while not caring about performance, sizing, static code analysis, or security data.

On the other hand, we could establish a user-acceptance test, or pre-production environment, where our pipeline filter will only accept upgrades and updates that are part of an actual contract (such as EULAs that filter requests, as illustrated below) that we've signed with a specific vendor. We would thereby be assured that anything received has been tested properly and is appropriately secure for deployment.

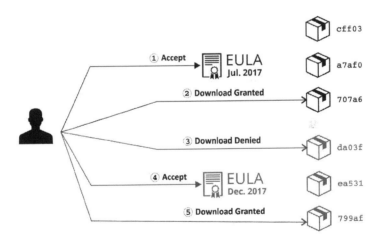

Filtering the Pipeline with a EULA

With so much information available, we could design our own pre-production filters. We could, for example, screen our pipeline for a new standard that we're hoping to see, or elaborate potential outcomes from the execution of our own in-house tests.

With fully automated testing and validation already being accomplished by the software producer – and those automation systems generating a wealth of highly specific and searchable information – it should also be much easier to design and automate user-side tests which would be configured to precisely match what we would be placing in production. This would actually be extremely desirable, because software consumers quite often use third-party handles, and even their own software, in very specific ways, requiring very specific types of setups, making use of very specific data to address very specific use cases. Such in-house testing would put consumers in a better position to provide highly detailed metadata information back to the software producer about the results of their own tests, strengthening the vendor's ability to improve their liquid software flows and provide more specifically tailored solutions.

CHAPTER 6:
WHAT'S NEXT?

*"If you know how to make software,
then you can create big things."*
— Xavier Niel, entrepreneur

It's Just the Way It Is

Humankind has repeatedly demonstrated that it can and will quickly accept, absorb, adapt, and ultimately advance useful new technologies. Millions of people who banged out their college papers on manual typewriters are still in the workforce. The first mass-market availability of a GUI-based computer was only a little over a generation ago. PDAs became a thing in the mid-to-late '90s. Then came portable digital media players, smartphones, and tablets. Now, we've entered the dawning era of IoT, AI-driven virtual assistants, mechatronics, and multi-agent systems. It's difficult for many among the typewriter alumni to even imagine how they got by in those BC (Before Computing) years. They speak digital fluently now, albeit with an accent. The generation in school now has never known anything *other* than a software-centric world where digital technologies aren't an add-on to life; they're a natural part of it.

We're right on the cusp of liquidity becoming an imperative. Major firms that have already developed and successfully deployed continuous update technologies are now open sourcing these to everyone. All the practices that have produced their innovations, once corporate secrets, are being mainstreamed. Soon enough, everyone will be saying, "It's just how we do things."

Through DevOps practices, liquefaction, and increasing standardization of processes, we'll keep reinventing software – reusing elements here, repurposing components there. There will be limberness to software that will make it ever easier to offer specific, custom-tailored solutions. Every piece of software being written today makes use of software components or codes that others made, or that your own company made and had used for a different project. Of course, reuse is only practical if recurring problems are being addressed. In this chain of dependency, as new software is being composed it's inevitable that a component borrowed from here will be used to break up a separate component somewhere else, which will result in the introduction of a new version (an upgrade). This type of development organically produces huge matrices of components, dependencies, and new features. Individuals cannot be expected to make choices from mountains of different reusable components, let alone verify which might contain compatibility or performance issues, vulnerabilities or bugs, or that might behave in any other undesirable way. All of this reuse, breaking, changing, and reinvention is simply beyond human capacity to manage.

Let the Machines Work

As continuous update and artificial intelligence (AI) systems mature, we may find that the evolution of liquid software will move beyond machine management and into machine *creation* of software. To obtain the best, feature-rich output possible, perhaps it will simply be enough to declare what dependencies we need without necessarily specifying particular versions.

In a perfected continuous update environment, we anticipate that pieces of code will be written before there is any demand or specific request for them, per se. We add that little caveat at the end because while no one will be texting or calling on the phone, a significant attribute of the liquid software environment is its inherent ability to automatically respond to "demands" or "requests" for new features by analyzing data flows coming from software that's already been deployed. As we design, create, and deploy more liquid software, we'll acquire more user activity data from an increasing number of continuous data flows. With more information, we'll be able to improve the way the machines that monitor this data accommodate user needs and desires. This type of virtuous cycle will result in faster production and distribution of ongoing improvements to software, which will result in enhanced user experiences.

From the perspective of developers, life will be easier and more productive. They will spend less time searching for problems, because the liquid environment will include continuous testing that generates real-world, real-use data. Developers won't need to intuit user needs and desires or to depend on anecdotal or limited survey data. They'll be able to see what users are doing and respond to their needs with greater specificity and speed than ever before.

Further on, software creation might become more human. There will be more use of natural language, visualizations, and direct, conversational interactions with machines. Development might be as simple as describing intent. For example, we might tell an AI-driven machine that we'd like to have a new program built or a database created that can attract a particular type of consumer. We'd then give our digital friend the task of finding the best stack that includes components for e-commerce, customer service, and so forth. We'd be able to create brand new things, whole new experiences – software mash-ups, if you please – from existing pieces, with very limited integration work. What once would have been entire projects that took weeks or months to execute could be accomplished in a matter of minutes.

Maybe in this environment, more people will actually think of themselves as software creators. Perhaps it will become commonplace for all types of companies to include a Director of Software Creation among its roster of employees. There won't be a high bar for technical rigor because machines will handle problems related to precision. More people will be able to use and create software in a more casual way.

Onward

Many of the concepts and approaches presented in this book are still new to the software industry. There are those in charge of corporate operations who are reluctant to consider a shift to continuous updates. Their qualms tend to arise from uncertainty about precisely what it will take to build a continuous update infrastructure within their own firms. In some quarters, the pushback is simply grounded in an unwillingness to adapt to new ways of thinking and doing things. Despite this, there are developers, IT and DevOps professionals everywhere who are now liquid software advocates. And having them among our ranks means we can say that the revolution has truly arrived!

Resistance to modernization ("Why?") inevitably gives way to generational shifts ("Why not?"). In our current moment, there are legacy development methodologies, legacy infrastructures, and legacy apps, which many companies are trying to maintain. But there just aren't enough engineers and developers to keep nursing all those legacies along. And while becoming liquid implies investments of time, energy, and money, it will be nothing in comparison to losing one's competitive edge to rivals and new entrants that have embraced continuous updates.

We acknowledge that there are those within the software industry who are concerned about the possibility of automation making their jobs obsolete. Never was it said better than by Pulitzer Prize-winning author, Upton Sinclair, while running for governor of California in 1934: "A man will never agree with something that threatens [his] income." We believe, however, that the liquid software wave is upon us and that we're in the midst of an unstoppable revolution. Only the job titles are changing, not the demand for people. As the software industry increasingly automates, what's changing is the way we work, not the numbers of people who are working.

Frankly, going liquid has never been easier. These days, storage, memory, and CPU are quite inexpensive. Entire databases can be easily backed up. Complete datasets can be active and accessible while duplicates are used to run parallel tests, production data environments, and platform validations. Our means of implementation are readily available and cost effective.

As we go liquid and witness a complete reboot of the infrastructure for software development, we should also consider implications beyond high-tech progress and bottom line efficiencies. Powerful new technologies can open up completely new scenarios, create entirely different categories of value, and solve problems we may not yet know exist.

If you now understand the promise of liquid software – make the case! If you've tried it in your own corner of the industry, but have come up against some resistance, don't give up! The more you can demonstrate that there is a way to execute continuous updates with zero downtime, which preserves data integrity in a secure, economical, and speedily accessible manner, the more likely and more quickly this revolution will transform the world!

REFERENCES in order of appearance

Pollard, C. William. *The soul of the firm*. Zondervan, 2000, p.114.

"Introducing Grafeas: An open-source API to audit and govern your software supply chain." *Grafeas*, Grafeas Authors, 12 Oct. 2017, grafeas.io/blog/introducing-grafeas.

Samit, Jay. *Disrupt yourself*. Pan Macmillan, 2015.

"Tech Talk: Linus Torvalds on Git." *YouTube*, Google, 14 May 2007, www.youtube.com/watch?v=4XpnKHJAok8.

Burt, Gabor George. "Pillow Concert: Design Offerings That Consumers Can Personalize Instead of Creating Ready-Made Ones." *The Economic Times* [Mumbai], 20 Sept. 2013, economictimes.indiatimes.com/magazines/corporate-dossier/pillow-concert-design-offerings-that-consumers-can-personalize-instead-of-creating-ready-made-ones/articleshow/22762138.cms.

Sabatini, Rafael. *Scaramouche: A romance of the French Revolution by Rafael Sabatini*. Project Gutenberg, 1 Nov. 1999, gutenberg.org/ebooks/1947.

Newman, Sam. *Building microservices: Designing fine-grained systems*. O'Reilly Media, Inc., 2015.

Haverbeke, Marijn. *Eloquent JavaScript: A modern introduction to programming*. No Starch Press, 2014.

Robinson, Edward. "Tech Billionaire Made in France Seeds Paris Entrepreneurs." *Bloomberg.com*, Bloomberg, 24 June 2014, www.bloomberg.com/news/articles/2014-06-24/tech-billionaire-made-in-france-seeds-paris-entrepreneurs.

ABOUT THE AUTHORS

Fred Simon

Fred is an avid software visionary with over 25 years of hands-on open source coding experience. He is a co-founder and the Chief Architect of JFrog, the DevOps accelerator company. He was also the founder of AlphaCSP – a Java experts consulting firm that was acquired in 2005. As a community influencer, Fred has been part of the most challenging changes in the software industry and has led Fortune 500 companies in their transition to DevOps. In 2015, Fred envisioned a world in which software is "liquid" and revealed the driving force behind the DevOps Revolution: Continuous Software Updates.

Yoav Landman

Yoav is a devout engineer, the creator of Artifactory, and a co-founder and Chief Technology Officer of JFrog. With over 20 years of experience as a Software Architect of enterprise applications, he plays a significant role in the evolution of DevOps. In 2006, Yoav created Artifactory as an open source project paving the way for the software community to a new domain of managing binaries. Prior to JFrog, Yoav created many production solutions as a consultant in the fields of Continuous Integration and Distributed Systems. He is also an accredited speaker and a Java Rockstar.

Baruch Sadogursky

Baruch is a vibrant and passionate advocate in the software development community. He is known as a champion in vocalizing key technical problems and offering inventive solutions in the high-tech industry. Baruch has been a software professional, consultant, architect and speaker for almost 20 years. He has been JFrog's Developer Advocate since 2012. Prior to JFrog, Baruch was an Innovation Expert at BMC Software and a consultant and software architect at AlphaCSP. Baruch is a Cloud Native Computing Foundation Ambassador, an Oracle Developer Champion, a Java Rockstar and a leading DevOps evangelist.

Made in the
USA
Lexington, KY